First World War
and Army of Occupation
War Diary
France, Belgium and Germany

5 DIVISION
13 Infantry Brigade
King's Own Scottish Borderers 2nd Battalion
and London Regiment 9th (County of London) Battalion
(Queen Victoria's Rifles)
4 August 1914 - 31 January 1916

WO95/1558

The Naval & Military Press Ltd
www.nmarchive.com
Published in association with The National Archives

Published by

The Naval & Military Press Ltd

Unit 10 Ridgewood Industrial Park,

Uckfield, East Sussex,

TN22 5QE England

Tel: +44 (0) 1825 749494

www.naval-military-press.com

www.nmarchive.com

This diary has been reprinted in facsimile from the original. Any imperfections are inevitably reproduced and the quality may fall short of modern type and cartographic standards.

Contents

Document type	Place/Title	Date From	Date To
Heading	WO95/1558/1		
Heading	5 Division 13 Bde 2 Bn. K.O.Y.L.I. 1914 Aug-1915 Dec To 32 Div 97 Bde.		
Heading	13th Brigade. 5th Division. 2nd Battalion King's Own Yorkshire Light Infantry August 1914.-Dec 1915.		
War Diary	Dublin	04/08/1914	14/08/1914
War Diary	At Sea	15/08/1914	15/08/1914
War Diary	Havre	16/08/1914	17/08/1914
War Diary	Amiens Busigny	18/08/1914	18/08/1914
War Diary	Maroilles	18/08/1914	21/08/1914
War Diary	Map B.T. Mons No. 2364	21/08/1914	21/08/1914
War Diary	Boussu	22/08/1914	31/08/1914
War Diary	Appendix (I) action of Le Cateau	26/08/1914	26/08/1914
Miscellaneous	Appendix II		
Miscellaneous	Lieut.-Colonel R.C. Bond. D.S.O. Nethergate House. Clare. Suffolk.	26/08/1914	26/08/1914
Miscellaneous	Diary. 2nd Battn: K.O. Yorkshire Light Infantry.		
Diagram etc	Le Cateau No. 1 Original Extension Of 2/K.O.Y.L.I. 5 a.m. 26th August 1914		
Diagram etc	Le Cateau No. 2 Original Extension Of 2/K.O.Y.L.I. 26 August 1914		
Miscellaneous	Historical Section, Committee Of Imperial Defence (Military Branch), Public Record Office Chancery Lane E.C.	11/07/1918	11/07/1918
Miscellaneous	P.A. Le Cateau Col. Bond 2/K.O.Y.L.I.	11/07/1918	11/07/1918
Miscellaneous	Rough Copy of Letter to Col Bond-105th		
Miscellaneous	Hotel Pension Kieviet Wassenaar Holland 17 May 1918	17/05/1918	17/05/1918
Miscellaneous	The "British News" Offices Amsterdam. July. 11.	11/07/1918	11/07/1918
Heading	13th Brigade. 5th Division. 2nd Battalion King's Own Yorkshire Light Infantry September 1914.		
War Diary	Crepy	01/09/1914	13/09/1914
War Diary	Les Cammieres	14/09/1914	14/09/1914
War Diary	Les Cammieres-La Cobinne Wood	15/09/1914	15/09/1914
War Diary	La Gobinne Wood	16/09/1914	24/09/1914
War Diary	Missy	25/09/1914	30/09/1914
Miscellaneous	Appendix II		
Heading	13th Brigade. 5th Division. 2nd Battalion King's Own Yorkshire Light Infantry October 1914.		
War Diary	Missy	01/10/1914	01/10/1914
War Diary	Vasseny	02/10/1914	02/10/1914
War Diary	Violaine	03/10/1914	03/10/1914
War Diary	Hartennes	04/10/1914	04/10/1914
War Diary	Lagny	05/10/1914	06/10/1914
War Diary	Fresnoy	07/10/1914	07/10/1914
War Diary	Abbeville	08/10/1914	08/10/1914
War Diary	Gueschart	09/10/1914	09/10/1914
War Diary	Haravesnes	10/10/1914	10/10/1914
War Diary	Valhuon	11/10/1914	11/10/1914
War Diary	Vandricourt	12/10/1914	12/10/1914
War Diary	N & Q in Annequin	13/10/1914	14/10/1914

War Diary	Le Hamel	15/10/1914	16/10/1914
War Diary	Richebourg L'Avoue	17/10/1914	17/10/1914
War Diary	Trenches Lannoy	18/10/1914	20/10/1914
War Diary	Bois De Biez	21/10/1914	21/10/1914
War Diary	Lorgies	22/10/1914	22/10/1914
War Diary	Trenches Richebourg L'Avoue	23/10/1914	25/10/1914
War Diary	Richebourg L'Avoue (Near Bethune)	26/10/1914	01/11/1914
Heading	2nd Bn. King's Own Yorkshire Lieut Infantry In France. October To December 1914.		
Miscellaneous	Copy Of Letter Dated "In France With 2nd Bn. K.O.Y.L.I. 16th October 1914" Form 5216 Sergeant E.T. Richards, 2nd Bn. Koyli Koyli To Captain H.W.B. Thorp, K.O.Y.L.I.	16/02/1914	16/02/1914
Heading	13th Brigade. 5th Division. 2nd Battalion King's Own Yorkshire Light Infantry November 1914.		
War Diary		01/11/1914	21/11/1914
War Diary	Locre	22/11/1914	26/11/1914
War Diary	Locre To Neuve Eglise.	27/11/1914	27/11/1914
War Diary	Trenches	28/11/1914	30/11/1914
Heading	13th Brigade. 5th Division. 2nd Battalion King's Own Yorkshire Light Infantry December 1914.		
War Diary	Trenches	01/12/1914	03/12/1914
War Diary	Trenches To St Jans Cappell	04/12/1914	04/12/1914
War Diary	Billets	05/12/1914	09/12/1914
War Diary	Trenches East Of Linden Hoek	10/12/1914	10/12/1914
War Diary	Trenches	11/12/1914	13/12/1914
War Diary	Lindenhoek	14/12/1914	14/12/1914
War Diary	Near Linden Hoek	15/12/1914	16/12/1914
War Diary	Dranoutre	17/12/1914	18/12/1914
War Diary	Trenches	19/12/1914	21/12/1914
War Diary	Lindenhoek	22/12/1914	22/12/1914
War Diary	St. Jans Cappel	23/12/1914	28/12/1914
War Diary	To Trenches On River Douve	29/12/1914	29/12/1914
War Diary	Trenches	30/12/1914	31/12/1914
Heading	13th Brigade. 5th Division. 2nd Battalion King's Own Yorkshire Light Infantry January 1915.		
War Diary	At Neuve Eglise	01/01/1915	06/01/1915
War Diary	Neuve Eglise To Trenches In Sector B.	06/01/1915	06/01/1915
War Diary	In Trenches ? Sector B.	07/01/1915	07/01/1915
War Diary	Trenches.	08/01/1915	08/01/1915
War Diary	To Neuve Eglise	09/01/1915	09/01/1915
War Diary	To Bailleul	10/01/1915	10/01/1915
War Diary	Bailleul	11/01/1915	15/01/1915
War Diary	To Dranoutre	16/01/1915	16/01/1915
War Diary	At Dranoutre	17/01/1915	17/01/1915
War Diary	Dranoutre To Trenches In Sector D.	18/01/1915	18/01/1915
War Diary	Trenches In Sector D.	19/01/1915	20/01/1915
War Diary	To Dranoutre	21/01/1915	21/01/1915
War Diary	Dranoutre	22/01/1915	22/01/1915
War Diary	To Trenches In Sector D.	23/01/1915	23/01/1915
War Diary	Trenches To Bailleul.	24/01/1915	24/01/1915
War Diary	Bailleul	25/01/1915	31/01/1915
Heading	13th Bde. 5th Div. Attached To 28th Div From 19.2.15. 2nd K.O.Y.L.I. February 1915.		
War Diary	Baill Eul To Trenches	01/02/1915	01/02/1915
War Diary	Trenches	02/02/1915	09/02/1915

War Diary	Baill Eul	10/02/1915	15/02/1915
War Diary	At Bailleul	16/02/1915	19/02/1915
War Diary	To Ouderdom.	19/02/1915	19/02/1915
War Diary	Trenches Near Verbranden Molen	20/02/1915	24/02/1915
War Diary	Support Trenches At Blaauwpoort	25/02/1915	25/02/1915
War Diary	Trenches To Vlamertinghe	26/02/1915	26/02/1915
War Diary	Vlamertinghe	27/02/1915	28/02/1915
Heading	13th Bde. 5th Div. 13th Bde. 5th Div. 2nd K.O.Y.L.I. 1915.		
Heading	13th Bde. 5th Div. Attached To 28 Div. 2nd K.O.Y.L.I. March 1915.		
War Diary	To Trenches At Verbranden Molen	01/03/1915	02/03/1915
War Diary	To Ypres	03/03/1915	03/03/1915
War Diary	At Ypres	04/03/1915	04/03/1915
War Diary	To Trenches	05/03/1915	05/03/1915
War Diary	Trenches At Verbranden Molen	06/03/1915	06/03/1915
War Diary	Ypres	07/03/1915	08/03/1915
War Diary	Trenches At Verbranden Molen	09/03/1915	09/03/1915
War Diary	Trenches To Reserve Near Verbranden Molen	10/03/1915	10/03/1915
War Diary	Reserve At Vlamertinghe	11/03/1915	13/03/1915
War Diary	Vlamertinghe To St. Eloi	14/03/1915	14/03/1915
War Diary	St Eloi	15/03/1915	16/03/1915
War Diary	Support Trenches At Resenttal Chakan	16/03/1915	16/03/1915
War Diary	Trenches In Sector A	18/03/1915	19/03/1915
War Diary	To/K Ruistraat	20/03/1915	20/03/1915
War Diary	At K Ruistraat	21/03/1915	21/03/1915
War Diary	To Trenches In Sector A.	22/03/1915	23/03/1915
War Diary	Support at Rosenttal	24/03/1915	24/03/1915
War Diary	At/Rosenttal	25/03/1915	25/03/1915
War Diary	Rosenttal To Vlamertinghe	26/03/1915	26/03/1915
War Diary	At Vlamertinghe	27/03/1915	30/03/1915
War Diary	Trenches	31/03/1915	31/03/1915
War Diary	13th Bde. 5th Div. 2nd K.O.Y.L.I. 1915.		
Heading	13th Brigade. 28th Division (Brigade Returned To 5th Division 7.4.15.) 2nd Battalion King's Own Yorkshire Light Infantry April 1915.		
War Diary	Trenches At Verbranden Molen	01/04/1915	07/04/1915
War Diary	Trenches	07/04/1915	10/04/1915
War Diary	Reninghelst.	11/04/1915	16/04/1915
War Diary	Ypres	17/04/1915	17/04/1915
War Diary	Hill 60	18/04/1915	19/04/1915
War Diary	To Ouderdom Huts	20/04/1915	20/04/1915
War Diary	At Ouderdom	21/04/1915	21/04/1915
War Diary	Ouderdom Towards Ypres	22/04/1915	22/04/1915
War Diary	Attached To 1st Canadian Divn. In Operation N.E. Of Ypres.	23/04/1915	24/04/1915
War Diary	With Canadian Divn.	25/04/1915	28/04/1915
War Diary	Attached To 1st Canadian Divn.	29/04/1915	03/05/1915
Miscellaneous	Address To Bn. By Bn-Genl. Wanlen O" Gowan 21/04/15	21/04/1915	21/04/1915
Miscellaneous	Address To 13th Infty Bde (Order Regts Attached)	22/04/1915	22/04/1915
Heading	13th Bde. 5th Div. 2nd K.O.Y.L.I. May 1915.		
Miscellaneous	Attached To 1 Canadian Div. April 29.		
War Diary	Attached To 1st Canadian Div.	01/05/1915	04/05/1915
War Diary	Rejoined 5th Divn.	05/05/1915	06/05/1915
War Diary	Attack On Zwarteleen Salient.	06/05/1915	07/05/1915

War Diary	Railway Gutakat Near Zillebeeke	08/05/1915	10/05/1915
War Diary	To Hub At Sapper Town.	11/05/1915	11/05/1915
War Diary	Sapper Town	12/05/1915	12/05/1915
War Diary	Sapper Town Hub	13/05/1915	16/05/1915
War Diary	Zillebeke Pond.	17/05/1915	19/05/1915
War Diary	To Sapper Town	20/05/1915	20/05/1915
War Diary	At Sapper Town.	21/05/1915	24/05/1915
War Diary	Sapper Town.	25/05/1915	25/05/1915
War Diary	To Trenches At St Eloi	26/05/1915	26/05/1915
War Diary	St. Eloi.	27/05/1915	28/05/1915
War Diary	Dickebush Huts	29/05/1915	31/05/1915
Heading	13th Bde. 5th Div. 2nd K.O.Y.L.I. June. 1915.		
War Diary	Dickebush L to St Eloi Defences	01/06/1915	01/06/1915
War Diary	Trenches At St Eloi	02/06/1915	06/06/1915
War Diary	Dickebusch Huts	07/06/1915	09/06/1915
War Diary	Dickebush Huts to Trenches At St Eloi.	09/06/1915	09/06/1915
War Diary	Trenches At St Eloi.	10/05/1916	15/05/1916
War Diary	St Eloi To Dickebush Hub	16/05/1916	16/05/1916
War Diary	Dickebush Huts	17/06/1915	18/06/1915
War Diary	St Eloi Defences.	19/06/1915	24/06/1915
War Diary	To Dickebush Hub.	25/06/1915	25/06/1915
War Diary	Dickebush Huts	26/06/1915	27/06/1915
War Diary	St Eloi Defenses	28/06/1915	03/07/1915
Heading	13th Bde. 5th Div. 2nd K.O.Y.L.I. July. 1915.		
War Diary	St. Eloi Defences	01/07/1915	03/07/1915
War Diary	St. Eloi Defenses To Dickebush Huts.	04/07/1915	04/07/1915
War Diary	Dickebush Huts	05/07/1915	06/07/1915
War Diary	Dickebush Huts To Trenches At St Eloi	07/07/1915	07/07/1915
War Diary	Trenches At St Eloi	08/07/1915	12/07/1915
War Diary	Trenches St Eloi To Dickebush Huts.	13/07/1915	13/07/1915
War Diary	Dickebush Huts	14/07/1915	15/07/1915
War Diary	To St Eloi Trenches.	16/07/1915	16/07/1915
War Diary	St Eloi Trenches	17/07/1915	20/07/1915
War Diary	St Eloi Trenches To Rosen Hill Camp Near Zevecoten.	21/07/1915	21/07/1915
War Diary	Rosen Hill Camp To Steenvoorde.	22/07/1915	22/07/1915
War Diary	Steen Voorde.	23/07/1915	30/07/1915
War Diary	Steen Voorde To La Neu Ville.	31/07/1915	31/07/1915
Heading	13th Bde. 5th Div. 2nd K.O.Y.L.I. August 1915		
War Diary	At La Neuville.	01/08/1915	01/08/1915
War Diary	La Neuville.	02/08/1915	02/08/1915
War Diary	La Neuville To Ribemont.	03/08/1915	03/08/1915
War Diary	Ribemont To Bronfray.	04/08/1915	04/08/1915
War Diary	Bronfay Farm	05/08/1915	14/08/1915
War Diary	Bronfray To Trenches At Carnoy	15/08/1915	15/08/1915
War Diary	Trenches At Carnoy	16/08/1915	23/08/1915
War Diary	Trenches To Bronfray. Fm.	24/08/1915	24/08/1915
War Diary	Bronfray.	25/08/1915	31/08/1915
Heading	13th Bde. 5th Div. 2nd K.O.Y.L.I. September. 1915		
War Diary	Bronfray Farm To Trenches At Carnoy.	01/09/1915	01/09/1915
War Diary	Trenches At Carnoy.	02/09/1915	08/09/1915
War Diary	Trenches To Bray.	09/09/1915	09/09/1915
War Diary	Bray	10/09/1915	16/09/1915
War Diary	To Trenches At Carnoy.	17/09/1915	17/09/1915
War Diary	Trenches At Carnoy	18/09/1915	22/09/1915
War Diary	Trenches To Bray	23/09/1915	23/09/1915
War Diary	Bray.	24/09/1915	30/09/1915

Heading	13th Bde. 5th Div. 2nd K.O.Y.L.I. October.1915		
War Diary	Bray.	01/10/1915	01/10/1915
War Diary	Bray-Bronfray.	02/10/1915	02/10/1915
War Diary	Bray & Bronfray	03/10/1915	07/10/1915
War Diary	Bronfray.	08/10/1915	08/10/1915
War Diary	Bronfray & Billon	09/10/1915	09/10/1915
War Diary	Trenches At Carnoy	10/10/1915	13/10/1915
War Diary	To Bray.	14/10/1915	14/10/1915
War Diary	To Sailly Lorette	15/10/1915	15/10/1915
War Diary	At Sailly Lorette	16/10/1915	20/10/1915
War Diary	To Bray.	21/10/1915	21/10/1915
War Diary	Bray	22/10/1915	25/10/1915
War Diary	Bray To Trenches At Carnoy	26/10/1915	26/10/1915
War Diary	Trenches At Carnoy	27/10/1915	31/10/1915
Heading	13th Bde. 5th Div. 2nd K.O.Y.L.I. 1915		
Heading	13th Bde. 5th Div. 2nd K.O.Y. L.I. November. 1915		
War Diary	Trenches At Carnoy	01/11/1915	01/11/1915
War Diary	Bronfay And Billon Wood	02/11/1915	06/11/1915
War Diary	Trenches At Carnoy	07/11/1915	13/11/1915
War Diary	Bray	14/11/1915	19/11/1915
War Diary	Trenches At Carnoy	20/11/1915	26/11/1915
War Diary	Bronfay And Billon	27/11/1915	30/11/1915
Miscellaneous	Report By Intelligence Officer 2/K.O.Y.L.I.	10/11/1915	10/11/1915
Miscellaneous	Report By Intelligence Officer 2/K.O.Y.L.I.	08/11/1915	08/11/1915
Miscellaneous	Report By Intelligence Officer 2/K.O.Y.L.I.	11/11/1915	11/11/1915
Miscellaneous	Report By Intelligence Officer 2/K.O.Y.L.I.	12/11/1915	12/11/1915
Miscellaneous	Report By Intelligence Officer 2/K.O.Y.L.I.	13/11/1915	13/11/1915
Miscellaneous	Report By Intelligence Officer 2/K.O.Y.L.I.	20/11/1915	20/11/1915
Miscellaneous	Intelligence Report By J.O. 2/K.O.Y.L.I.	21/11/1915	21/11/1915
Miscellaneous	Report By Intelligence Officer 2/K.O.Y.L.I. Sub. Sector B2	22/11/1915	22/11/1915
Miscellaneous	Report By Intelligence Officer 2/ K.O.Y.L.I. Sub Sector B2	23/11/1915	23/11/1915
Miscellaneous	Report By Intelligence Officer 2/K.O.Y.L.I. Sub Sector B2	24/11/1915	24/11/1915
Miscellaneous	Report By Intelligence Officer 2/K.O.Y.L.I. Sub Sector B2	25/11/1915	25/11/1915
Heading	13th Bde. 5th Div. Transferred To 97th Bde. 32nd Division 25.12.15. 2nd K.O.Y.L.I. December 1915		
War Diary	Trenches At Carnoy	01/12/1915	07/12/1915
War Diary	Bray	08/12/1915	11/12/1915
War Diary	Trenches At Carnoy	12/12/1915	15/12/1915
War Diary	Froissy Huts	16/12/1915	18/12/1915
War Diary	Bronfay And Billon	19/12/1915	19/12/1915
War Diary	Trenches At Carnoy	20/12/1915	23/12/1915
War Diary	Bray	24/12/1915	27/12/1915
War Diary	Froissy Huts	28/12/1915	28/12/1915
War Diary	Sailly, Lorette	29/12/1915	29/12/1915
War Diary	Albert	30/12/1915	30/12/1915
War Diary	Bouzincourt	31/12/1915	31/12/1915
Heading	WO95/1558/2		
Heading	5 Division 13 Bde 9 Bn London Regt 1914 Oct-1916 Jan To 56 Div-169 BBE		
Heading	13th Brigade. 5th Division. Disembarked Havre 5.11.14. Joined 13th Brigade 27.11.14. 9th Battalion The London Regiment 18.10.14 To 3.1.15. Jan1916		

War Diary	Fleet To Eastleigh	18/10/1914	29/10/1914
War Diary	Winchester	30/10/1914	30/10/1914
War Diary	Southampton.	31/10/1914	04/11/1914
War Diary	Havre.	05/11/1914	06/11/1914
War Diary	St Omer.	07/11/1914	07/11/1914
War Diary	Arcques.	08/11/1914	19/11/1914
War Diary	Hazebrouck.	20/11/1914	20/11/1914
War Diary	Bailleul	21/11/1914	27/11/1914
War Diary	Neuve Eglise.	29/11/1914	11/12/1914
War Diary	Dranoutre.	12/12/1914	23/12/1914
War Diary	St Jan's Cappel	27/12/1914	29/12/1914
War Diary	Neuve Eglise	30/12/1914	03/01/1915
Heading	13th Bde. 5th Div. 9th London Regt. January To December 1915		
War Diary		01/01/1915	31/01/1915
Heading	13th Bde. 5th Div. 9th London Regt. February 1915		
War Diary	Bailleul	01/02/1915	01/02/1915
War Diary	Dranoutre.	02/02/1915	09/02/1915
War Diary	Bailleul.	10/02/1915	19/02/1915
War Diary	Dranoutre	20/02/1915	28/02/1915
Heading	13th Bde. 5th Div. 9th London Regt. March 1915		
War Diary	Dranoutre	01/03/1915	11/03/1915
War Diary	St Jans Capel	12/03/1915	14/03/1915
War Diary	Ploegsteert	17/03/1915	17/03/1915
War Diary	Bailleul	18/03/1915	22/03/1915
War Diary	Ypres	23/03/1915	26/03/1915
War Diary	Near Ouderdom.	27/03/1915	31/03/1915
Heading	13th Bde. 5th Div. 9th London Regt. April 1915		
Heading	13th Brigade 9th London (2 Y's Rifles). Vol V 1-30.4.15.		
War Diary	Ypres	01/04/1915	10/04/1915
War Diary	Ouderdom	11/04/1915	18/04/1915
War Diary	Ypres	19/04/1915	22/04/1915
War Diary	Elverdinghe	23/04/1915	30/04/1915
Miscellaneous	Key To Sketch.	09/04/1915	09/04/1915
Diagram etc	Zillebeke		
Diagram etc	Scale About 1/5000.		
Diagram etc			
Heading	13th Bde. 5th Div. 9th London Regt. May 1915		
War Diary	G 6. a & b	01/05/1915	03/05/1915
War Diary	Zevecoten	04/05/1915	04/05/1915
War Diary	Ouderdom.	05/05/1915	05/05/1915
War Diary	I 21. b.	06/05/1915	13/05/1915
War Diary	Scherpenberg	13/05/1915	19/05/1915
War Diary	Ouderdom.	20/05/1915	21/05/1915
War Diary	Chateau Blanc	22/05/1915	25/05/1915
War Diary	Voormezeele	26/05/1915	31/05/1915
Heading	13th Bde. 5th Div. 9th London Regt. June 1915		
War Diary	Voormezeele I.31.c	01/06/1915	30/06/1915
Heading	13th Bde. 5th Div. 9th London Regt. July 1915		
War Diary	Voormezeele I 31 (c)	01/07/1915	21/07/1915
War Diary	Reninghelst G.34.b	22/07/1915	22/07/1915
War Diary	Steenvoorde	23/07/1915	30/07/1915
War Diary	On Bail	31/07/1915	31/07/1915
Heading	13th Bde. 5th Div. 9th London Regt. August 1915		
War Diary	Laneuville	01/08/1915	02/08/1915

War Diary	La Neuville To Ribemont	03/08/1915	03/08/1915
War Diary	Ribemont To Bray Sur Somme	04/08/1915	04/08/1915
War Diary	Bray	05/08/1915	14/08/1915
War Diary	Bray To Bronfay	15/08/1915	15/08/1915
War Diary	Bronfay	16/08/1915	17/08/1915
War Diary	Bronfay To Carnoy	18/08/1915	18/08/1915
War Diary	Carnoy	19/08/1915	31/08/1915
Heading	13th Bde. 5th Div. 9th London Regt. September 1915		
War Diary	Bray & Carnoy	01/09/1915	22/09/1915
War Diary	H.Q. At Bronfay Farm	23/09/1915	30/09/1915
Heading	13th Bde. 5th Div. 9th London Regt. October 1915		
War Diary	Chipilly	01/10/1915	07/10/1915
War Diary	Bray & Etineham	08/10/1915	09/10/1915
War Diary	Bray & Carnoy	10/10/1915	31/10/1915
Heading	13th Bde. 5th Div. 9th London Regt. November 1915		
War Diary	Bray & Carnoy.	01/11/1915	30/11/1915
Heading	13th Bde. 5th Div. 9th London Regt. December 1915.		
War Diary	Bray & Carnoy	01/12/1915	30/12/1915
Heading	13th Brigade. 5th Division. Battalion Transferred To 169th Brigade. 56th Division 1st February 1916 War Diary 1/9th Battalion London Regiment (Q.V.R.) January 1916		
Heading	1/9 London Regt. Jan Vol XIV To 169 Bde Feby 1st 16.		
War Diary	Bray & Carnoy	01/01/1916	12/01/1916
War Diary	Sailly Laurette	13/01/1916	29/01/1916
War Diary	La Houssoye	30/01/1916	30/01/1916
War Diary	Talmas	31/01/1916	31/01/1916

WO 95/1558/1

5 DIVISION

13 BDE

2 BN K O Y L I

1914 AUG — 1915 DEC

TO 32 DIV 97 BDE

13th Brigade.

5th Division.

2nd BATTALION

KING'S OWN YORKSHIRE LIGHT INFANTRY

AUGUST 1914.

—

Dec 1915

Army Form C. 2118.

Instructions regarding War Diaries and Intelligence Summaries are contained in F. S. Regs., Part II. and the Staff Manual respectively. Title pages will be prepared in manuscript.

WAR DIARY
or
INTELLIGENCE SUMMARY.
(*Erase heading not required.*)

2nd Bn King's Own Yorkshire Light Infantry

Hour, Date, Place	Summary of Events and Information	Remarks and references to Appendices
5 20 pm August 4th 1914 DUBLIN	Order received by telephone message from Garrison Adjutant DUBLIN MOBILIZE	
5 25 pm	Orders issued to Battalion to mobilize	
7 30 pm	Telegraphed to War Office saying 3 Captains & Major on Battalion required to complete	
1 30 am August 5th DUBLIN	Telegram received from 13th Inf Bde "War has broken out with GERMANY"	
[illegible] 12 noon	Battalion medically examined 1 Officer (Lt PERKINS [illegible]) and 17 Rank & file found unfit. Strength of Battalion (without reservists) ready to take the field with the Battalion 18 Officers 450 R & F. Battalion garrisons [illegible] 3 DUBLIN DEFENCE SCHEME with strength of 3 officers 82 R & F. Officers from Special Reserve Battalion joined Captain [illegible] and Lieut HAYES for duty with DUBLIN Details [illegible] [illegible] for duty with Battalion these officers not included in above strength	
Aug 6th DUBLIN	2nd Day of mobilization 7 Officers 19 Sergeants 576 R & F [illegible] to complete [illegible] to war establishment [illegible]	
Aug 7th DUBLIN	3rd Day of mobilization Captain [illegible] MVO [illegible] [illegible] from Depot of 306 Reservists [illegible] to Depot at night. Strength of Bn [illegible]	

Instructions regarding War Diaries and Intelligence Summaries are contained in F. S. Regs., Part II. and the Staff Manual respectively. Title pages will be prepared in manuscript.

WAR DIARY
2nd Bn YORKSHIRE LIGHT INFANTRY
INTELLIGENCE SUMMARY.
(*Erase heading not required.*)

Army Form C. 2118.

Hour, Date, Place	Summary of Events and Information	Remarks and references to Appendices
Continued 5 pm Aug 7th 1914 DUBLIN	Telephone message received "This Div embarks 9 August" from BRIGADIER	ena Capt [illegible]
	MAJOR CALTATE left for the WAR OFFICE for staff appointment	
	Major HEATHCOTE and LIEUT [illegible] arrived for duty with battalion	
	Captain [illegible] and [illegible] PERRY and BROWNE left and [illegible] Depot for duty on mobilization	
1 am Aug 8th 1914 DUBLIN	4th Day of MOBILIZATION. LIEUTS SMYTH and [illegible] arrived with draft from Depot of 262 Reservists. The officers returned to Depot at night after handing over the men.	
2 pm	Battalion paraded fully mobilized (except [illegible] draft harness) for inspection by C.O.	
	Telephone message received "Military Sec War office [illegible] war establishment of Battalion increased by one Captain and 2 subalterns ordered to depot yesterday. 13th Inf Brigade	
6 pm	Telephone message received Ref [illegible] 13th Inf Bde instructions for embarkation. Dated 7th August. Embarkation of Bde postponed until Thursday 13th August. 13th Inf Bde 6 Officers and 40 R.F. required to complete	
Aug 9th 1914 Dublin	Major CALTATE rejoined Bn also Lieut Dawson and Captain L Simpson M.V.O.	
	3 officers & 20 R.F. required to complete establishment	

(9 26 6) W 257—976 100,000 4/12 H W V 79/3298

Army Form C. [illegible]18.

Instructions regarding War Diaries and Intelligence Summaries are contained in F. S. Regs., Part II. and the Staff Manual respectively. Title pages will be prepared in manuscript.

WAR DIARY
or
~~INTELLIGENCE SUMMARY.~~

Kings Own Yorkshire Light Infantry

[illegible] Capt

(*Erase heading not required.*)

Hour, Date, Place	Summary of Events and Information	Remarks and references to Appendices
Aug 10th 1914 DUBLIN	Battalion as part of the 13th Infantry Brigade marched to Phoenix Park and was [illegible] by Brigadier General CUTHBERT Cmdg 13th I B. Battalion up to strength and fully mobilized except 3 officers and 6 sets of heavy draught harness. Great difficulty has been experienced in obtaining harness	[illegible] Capt [illegible]
Aug 11th 1914 DUBLIN	Battalion took part in a route march of about 10 miles with the 13th I B. The [illegible] [illegible] well. The Battalion is still short of 3 officers and 6 sets of heavy draught harness.	[illegible] Capt [illegible]
Aug 12th 1914 Dublin	All posts relieved by [illegible] ~~[illegible]~~ except one post ([illegible] [illegible]) which was relieved by Dublin [illegible]. Orders received for 1st [illegible] to pass O'Connell Bridge at 5 AM tomorrow. Captain R S LEDGARD 1st Yorkshire Regt [illegible] for duty with Battalion.	[illegible] Capt [illegible]
Aug 13th 1914 Dublin	Reveille 3 a.m. At 4 a.m. following telegram received "Your Bn will not be able to embark before 2.30 p.m. today as the boat has not arrived [illegible] Staff officer." The [illegible] [illegible] [illegible] [illegible] not before 6 p.m. [illegible] [illegible] [illegible] [illegible] [illegible] [illegible] [illegible] [illegible] [illegible] [illegible] [illegible] [illegible] to be [illegible]. [illegible] [illegible] [illegible] and [illegible] [illegible] [illegible] [illegible] Regt [illegible] for [illegible] to Battalion [illegible] [illegible] officers [illegible] [illegible] [illegible]	[illegible] Capt [illegible]

Instructions regarding War Diaries and Intelligence Summaries are contained in F. S. Regs., Part II. and the Staff Manual respectively. Title pages will be prepared in manuscript.

1st 3 pages [illegible] and sent to [illegible]

Army Form C. 2118.

WAR DIARY 2nd YORKSHIRE LIGHT INFANTRY

or

INTELLIGENCE SUMMARY.

(*Erase heading not required.*)

Hour, Date, Place	Summary of Events and Information	Remarks and references to Appendices
4.30 pm Aug 14th 1914 DUBLIN	Battalion paraded at 4.30 pm and marched to ALEXANDRA DOCKS and embarked in the transport S.S. BUTESHIRE with Headquarters 14th Infantry Brigade, 2nd MANCHESTER REGIMENT and a signal section.	
7.30 pm — " —	The ship sailed at 7.30 PM ([illegible] time). The ship was badly fitted for the accommodation of officers and men but well fitted for horses. Weather calm.	
Aug 15th 1914 at Sea	At sea. Weather calm.	
4.30 pm Aug 16th 1914 HAVRE	Ship arrived off HAVRE at 4.30 p.m. and remained outside the docks until 9.30 pm when she steamed into the docks arriving at 10.15 pm when the troops immediately disembarked.	
11 pm	At 11 pm received instructions to be ready to move by train at 12.30 AM tomorrow.	
12.30 AM Aug 17th 1914 HAVRE	[illegible] move by train postponed owing to the transport and horses not being off the ship. The [illegible] large [illegible] by [illegible] [illegible]	

(9 26 6) W257—976 100,000 4/12 H W V 79/3298

Army Form C. 2118.

Instructions regarding War Diaries and Intelligence Summaries are contained in F. S. Regs., Part II. and the Staff Manual respectively. Title pages will be prepared in manuscript.

WAR DIARY
or
~~INTELLIGENCE SUMMARY~~.

(Erase heading not required.)

2nd K.O.Y.L.I.

Hour, Date, Place	Summary of Events and Information	Remarks and references to Appendices
Monday Aug 17th 1914 HAVRE	At 3.45 pm Battalion marched to the railway station at HAVRE and entrained. The train left at 8.45 pm for AMIENS. Battalion complete in [illegible] transport.	[illegible]
Tuesday Aug 18th 1914 AMIENS BUSIGNY	Battalion arrived at AMIENS at about 6.30 AM and after a short delay proceeded to BUSIGNY arriving there at about 11 AM leaving there at 11.35 am for LANDRECIES arriving at about 12.30 pm where the Battalion detrained and after waiting [illegible] for the [illegible] proceeded by march route	
5 pm MAROILLES	at 4 pm to MAROILLES where they joined the 13th Infantry Brigade [illegible]. The Bn arrived at MAROILLES at [illegible] pm and went into billets. The billets were [illegible] the inhabitants were [illegible] to the troops. The Bn found [illegible] outposts [illegible] out of the village [illegible] River de SAMBRE	[illegible]
Wednesday Aug 19th 1914 MAROILLES	Battalion remained in billets at MAROILLES	[illegible]
Thursday Aug 20th 1914 MAROILLES	Battalion received orders to move tomorrow	[illegible]
Friday Aug 21st 1914	Battalion formed the Advanced Guard of the 13th Infantry Brigade and marched from MAROILLES at 6-30 AM. and proceeded via BERLAYMONT [illegible]	

(9 26 6) W 257—976 100,000 4/12 H W V 79/3298

Army Form C. 2118.

Instructions regarding War Diaries and Intelligence Summaries are contained in F. S. Regs., Part II. and the Staff Manual respectively. Title pages will be prepared in manuscript.

WAR DIARY
or
INTELLIGENCE SUMMARY.
2 R O Y L I

(Erase heading not required.)

Hour, Date, Place	Summary of Events and Information	Remarks and references to Appendices
Friday Aug 21st 1914 Continued Map B.T. MONS to 2364	–LA PORQUERIES – BAVAY to HOUDIN arriving at about 3.30 p.m. & went into billets. Two companies were on outpost duty (C & D Companies) holding a line BELLIGNIES (exclusive) – VERDEAU – TAISNIERES – crossroads W of RIEZ de ERELLE.	C.H.A. Capt. Capl
Saturday Aug 22nd 1914 BOUSSU	Division continues to march Northward. Orders received at about 12.30 a.m. for the Bn. [illegible] of 13 Inf Bde to march tomorrow at 8.15 a.m. via DOUR on HORNU. At 5 a.m. orders received to march [illegible] hours earlier. At about 7.25 a.m. battalion marched (less D Coy [illegible] whom it was impossible to get off the outposts in time and who followed on later) via ATHIS – DOUR to BOUSSU where the Bn. went into billets in a [illegible]. Very hard marching over the cobbles through the mining towns. Enthusiastic reception all along the route. Brigade is holding the line of the canal from LES HERBIERES – MARIETTE and has ~~two Bns on [illegible] support duty.~~	C.H.A. Capt. C.H.A. Capt. [illegible] C.H.A. Capt. [illegible]
Sunday August 23rd 1914 BOUSSU 1 pm	During the night 22/23rd 2 coys (A + B) [illegible] to hold themselves in readiness to support the outpost line. [illegible] of 22nd C. & D. [illegible] for the duty. Orders received for C. & D. Coys to move up close to outpost line in support [illegible] at ST. GHISLAIN. A & B Coys ordered to move [illegible] support [illegible]	

Instructions regarding War Diaries and Intelligence Summaries are contained in F. S. Regs., Part II. and the Staff Manual respectively. Title pages will be prepared in manuscript.

WAR DIARY

or

INTELLIGENCE ~~SUMMARY~~.

(Erase heading not required.)

Army Form C. 2118.

Hour, Date, Place	Summary of Events and Information	Remarks and references to Appendices
Sunday 23rd August (Continued)	Coys. remained in close support 300x behind canal bank until 5 pm when ~~Brigade~~ orders were received from Brigade to retire. C & D Coys then went up on to canal bank to cover retirement of [illegible] and K.O.S.B. Railway bridge was blown up about 8 pm but bridge at ST GHISLAIN failed to blow. Order came for Battalion to retire about 9 pm after dark. About 2 pm [illegible] 2Lieut PEPYS was killed & Pte BOFFEY [illegible] wounded [illegible] [illegible] had been doing admirable work with the machine guns [illegible] had been in the firing line all day	Letter Lt. Lordy
Monday 24th August	Bn. marched to fields in the vicinity of WASMES where it concentrated. Marched into WASMES where it arrived about 7 am. Ordered to take up a position with 2 Coys (A & B) in firing line & 2 in support. B Coy occupied an advanced position on a Coal Dump. A Coy being slightly in rear & to the left on the railway line. The Divisional Artillery did great execution throughout the day and were of the utmost assistance during the retirement. Orders to retire in direction of BAVAY received about 1.30 pm. The Battalion retiring in conformation with 3/Dukes on left and ~~[illegible]~~ [illegible] on right. Companies retiring from alternate flanks. The Division went into bivouac in a field beyond SW of BAVAY.	Letter Lt. Lordy
Tuesday 25th August	Division marched at 3 a.m. and went into bivouac immediately beyond 5 S.E. LE CATEAU	
Wednesday 26th August	During last night A & B Coys were on outpost duty. The Brigade stood to arms at 2.30 am and received orders to take up a rear guard position facing South with the town of LE CATEAU some 1000x on right front of the line. C & D in [illegible] line, ~~[illegible]~~ A & B support. At 6 am these orders were cancelled and orders to [illegible] to occupy the whole position for defence were received	
7 am to 4 pm	The battle of LE CATEAU Commences	See Appendix (1)
		See Appendix (2)

(9 26 6) W257—976 100,000 4/12 H W V $\frac{79}{3298}$

Instructions regarding War Diaries and Intelligence Summaries are contained in F. S. Regs., Part II. and the Staff Manual respectively. Title pages will be prepared in manuscript.

WAR DIARY
or
~~INTELLIGENCE SUMMARY~~.
(*Erase heading not required.*)

Army Form C. 2118.

Hour, Date, Place	Summary of Events and Information	Remarks and references to Appendices
Wednesday 26th August (continued) 4 pm	By 4 pm the whole division was in retreat and no attempt at reorganisation could be made until we reached LESTACCS where what was left of the Battalion collected in a field. Pouring rain and very cold.	[signature]
Thursday 27th August 12 midnight to 2 am	During the night Gen Sir C Fergusson & Gen Cuthbert were working with a crowd at LESTACCS to get the double line of guns, wagons, etc out of what looked like a hopeless tangle. The Brigade marched, everyone dead tired and wet through. Marched about 3 am to the village of JOLLEZY just beyond the Canal, where Brigade through ST QUENTIN. Major TREVOR Lieut HARDIMAN joined with some of the men left were billets. Major Trevor took over command of the Battalion and appointed Lieutenant WILLIAMS as Adjutant. Strength of Battn about 8Y officers & 320 other ranks. Battalion was reorganised into 2 companies (A & B) commanded by Maj HEATHCOTE with Lieut HARDIMAN, (C & D) commanded by Capt J E SIMPSON with 2Lieut SLINGSBY. Casualty report sent in to Brigade and to the Base.	[signature]
Friday 28th August 2 am	During last night orders were received that the position South of the Canal was to be entrenched during the morning. These orders were cancelled and fresh ones issued for the Division to continue its retreat Southwards via NOYON to a field just North of village of ST AUDAIN. Orders were received to bivouac there with the prospect of going into billets 4 miles off on the following day.	[signature]
Saturday 29th August	Remained in bivouac all day. & men had a good rest. Orders to march into billets at CARLPONT at 5.30 pm. After halting about every 100 yards orders received to sleep on the road just short of CARLPONT	[signature]
Sunday 30th August	Marched at 3 am to JAULZY on River AISNES where we went into billets. Major HEATHCOTE wounded on Monday 31 Aug	[signature]
Monday 31st August	Marched at 8 am via CHELLES – ST ETIENNE – PIERREFONDS – MARIENVAL to CREPY 23 miles and a very hot day. The Battalion marched splendidly & kept the road through a really trying march only 3 men falling out in spite of the fact that men of some other units were falling out in masses.	[signature]

APPENDIX I

Instructions regarding War Diaries and Intelligence Summaries are contained in F. S. Regs., Part II. and the Staff Manual respectively. Title pages will be prepared in manuscript.

~~WAR DIARY~~

or

~~INTELLIGENCE SUMMARY.~~

(Erase heading not required.)

Army Form C. 2118.

Hour, Date, Place		Summary of Events and Information	Remarks and references to Appendices
		Appendix (1) Action of LE CATEAU	
Wednesday 26th August	5 am	Reference War diary for 26th Orders to entrench and fight in position received. The Position was hurriedly entrenched, 2nd K.O.Y.L.I. being in the front line on the West of main CAUDRY - BEAUMONT road near the B in BRIQUETRIE, with the 14th Brigade on our immediate right and K.O.S.B. on our left.	
	5.30 am	The enemy opened artillery fire on the ~~left~~ extreme left, probably directed against our 4th Division, which we understand was in action some 10 miles off. Later on the enemy developed a strong attack against the Spur S. of LE CATEAU occupied by the 14th Brigade. The enemy could make very little headway to our immediate front owing to the much better position so that they concentrated most of their attention against our right. After some hours of very severe fighting the position fell into the enemy's hands thus rendering our position very precarious if not untenable. In the mean time our trenches had been subjected to a very heavy fire from Artillery, ~~rifle~~ infantry + Machine guns. The artillery fire was so heavy and so effective that our own guns could ~~not~~ make but little impression being vastly outnumbered. As soon as the right Spur fell these guns were enfiladed and those placed in close support of the infantry could not be got out of action.	
	3 pm	By this time the enemy had succeeded in ~~[illegible]~~ firmly establishing themselves on our right and it became evident that a general retirement was inevitable as all our trenches were subjected to a very heavy enfilade fire from infantry + machine guns and our own artillery was almost entirely out of action. As we afterwards learnt, the whole of the Bn. Staff had been killed earlier in the action by a shell bursting in the trench. The retirement was therefore effected very much later than would otherwise have been the case owing to no orders being received. It was largely owing to this that the Battalion suffered such heavy losses as not only were the trenches subjected to very heavy enfilade fire for some considerable time but also troops retiring up the glacis slope in the rear were subjected to terrific burst of fire from rifles, machine guns and artillery who could concentrate their whole attention on successive parties retiring, there being no answering fire.	

Scott Buckley

APPENDIX II ~~WAR DIARY~~

or

~~INTELLIGENCE SUMMARY~~.

(Erase heading not required.)

Army Form C. 2118.

Instructions regarding War Diaries and Intelligence Summaries are contained in F. S. Regs., Part II. and the Staff Manual respectively. Title pages will be prepared in manuscript.

Hour, Date, Place	Summary of Events and Information	Remarks and references to Appendices
	LIST of CASUALTIES incurred at LE CATEAU 26th August 1914	
	OFFICERS	
Name	Nature of Casualty	Remarks
Lt Col R. C. Bond D.S.O	~~Killed~~ W P	
Major C. A. L. Yate	Reported Killed	Since reported by War Office as living.
Captain L. Simpson	Dangerously Wounded & Missing	
Captain C. C. G. Luther	Reported Killed	
Captain W. H. Keppel	Reported Killed	
Captain C. H. Ackroyd	Killed	
Captain W. P. Gattacre	Killed	
Lieutenant C. H. Rowan	Killed	Since ~~not~~ promoted Captain
" B. N. Denison	Killed	Since promoted Captain
" W. H. G. W. Arnott	Reported Captured	
" T. Reynolds	Missing	
" P. C. Wynne	~~Reported~~ Killed W P	
2nd Lieut Y. B. Ford	Reported Killed	
2nd Lieut T. B. Butt	Seriously Wounded & Missing	
2nd Lieut H. B. Hebbert	Missing	
2nd Lieut Ritchie	Killed	
Capt Legard 19th P.W.O. Yorkshire Regt	Killed	
Lieut Y. B. Ford East Yorkshire Regt	Reported Killed	Since ~~[illegible]~~ reported at the Base.

Total

Officers	Sergeants	Corporals	Buglers	Privates	Total
18	21	22	7	532	600

(9 26 6) W 257—976 100,000 4/12 H W V 79/3298

From LIEUT.-COLONEL R. C. BOND, D.S.O.,
NETHERGATE HOUSE,
CLARE, SUFFOLK.

Re The Battle of LE CATEAU
26 August 1914.

Though the LE CATEAU – CAMBRAI road itself in the neighbourhood of the BAVAI – REUMONT road, which crosses it ½ a mile West of LE CATEAU, had for hours been in the hands of the Germans, no further advance could be made by them here before 4.30 p.m. Up to that hour the trenches on both sides of the BAVAI road were contested by the 2nd. Battalion K.O.Y.L.I.

R.C. Bond
Lt-Col.

P.G. Letter Corr Diary
2/KOYLI August 1914
[illegible]

Copy No. 3.

DIARY.

2ND BATTN: K.O.YORKSHIRE LIGHT INFANTRY.

1914.

14th August. Marched to NORTH WALL, DUBLIN, at 4.0.pm, from PORTOBELLO BARRACKS. Embarkation commenced at 5.0.pm, on the S.S. "BUTESHIRE". Under weigh about 7.0.pm. Brigadier-General ROLT in Command. A Battalion of the MANCHESTER REGIMENT, (14th Brigade), also on board.

15th August. At sea all day. Destination believed to be LE HAVRE, but doubtful. Off LAND'S END we fell in with about a dozen Transports. H.M.S."GIBRALTAR", or a sister ship, passed us steaming N.W. and signalled "Good Luck".

16th August. Weather calm and hot. Short service held at mid-day. H.M.THE KING'S and LORD KITCHENER'S messages read to the Troops. Off the CHANNEL ISLANDS sighted six Submarines and a Dreadnought (French). Forced to lie to while we were overhauled by a French Torpedo-boat. LE HAVRE sighted at 2.0.pm. Lay to outside until 9.30.pm. Work of disembarkation began at 11.0.pm and proceeded all night. The Battalion lay down in a huge shed by the quay.

17th August. Waiting for orders till 1.0.pm. Marched about 2 miles to the station. Entrained about 5.0.pm. Train started about 6.30.pm.

18th August. Passed through ROUEN at night; AMIENS in the early morning. Arrived at LANDRECIES (our destination) at mid-day. The train was met by Captain STOURTON, (K.O.Y.L.I.). The Battalion was halted in a disused Cavalry barracks for the mid-day meal.

18th August. continued. Marched to MAROILLES in the afternoon, about 5 miles. The remaining three Battalions of the 13th Brigade were already there. The Brigadier, General CUTHBERT, met us in LANDRECIES. The position of the Battalion was N. and N.E. of the village, overlooking the RIVER SAMBRE. The Bridges were held by French Territorial Infantry.

19th August. Short route-march in the morning. We were given to expect a halt of 10 days at least. Companies on Out-post were B, (Major YATE) on the right, on the road to NOYELLES, and D, (Major TREVOR) on the left, on the road leading to the forrest of MORMAL.

20th August. Only the Infantry of the Division had so far been assembled; the first signs of Artillery were observable in the afternoon. Sir Charles FERGUSSON, Commanding the 5th Division, addressed each Battalion in turn, in a stirring speech. He said that any day now, tomorrow for instance, we might be in actual contact with the Enemy forces. That there must be no surrendering, and that men must fight to the last, with their fists if their rifles were useless. That he would be found with them in the last ditch. Confidential orders for a march tomorrow were received in the evening.

21st August. Marched from MAROILLES at 6.0.am. The Battalion was in Advance guard. C Company found the advanced party. Crossed the SAMBRE into the Forrest of MORMAL. At the five cross-roads, we headed for BERLAIMONT, thence to BAVAI by the main road. Halted at 12 noon for one hour. In BAVAI received orders to take up out-post line HOUDAIN-TAISNIÈRES, (the latter overlooking the

21st August. continued. field of MALPLAQUET). "C" (LUTHER) and "D" (TREVOR) Coys on out-post, the latter on the right. Heard tonight of Prussian Cavalry being in contact with our Cavalry Division between BRUSSELS and MONS. Orders for tomorrows march came at mid-night.

22nd August. (Saturday). Marched from HOUDAIN about 7.30.am. The Advance Guard Battalion being late, the Div: General ordered the K.O.Y.L.I. to take their place. Crossed the Belgian Frontier at 9.0.am. At 2.20.pm passed BOUSSU station and halted in a large meadow North of the railway line. Officers were sent out to reconnoitre the MONS-CONDÊ Canal. Later two Battalions of the Brigade, (K.O.S.BORDERERS and W.KENTS) proceeded on out-post duty along the Canal bank. The W.KENTS were on the right, with W.RIDING Battalion in support of them. The K.O.S.B's on the left with K.O.Y.L.I. in support at the Brewery. The Battalion Machine guns (under Lieut PEPYS) were moved forward to the Canal bank, between the forward Battalions, to strengthen the line.

23rd August. (Sunday). Morning spent in preparations and reconnaissance. At 11.0.am a conference of Battalion Commanders at Brigade Head-Quarters. at which it was arranged to relieve the battalions in the first line at 6 p.m. every 24 hours. During the preparation of the men's dinner, three shrapnel shells burst over the field outside the brewery building, wounding one man. Other shells burst over the outskirts of the town. Dinners were hurried through. "C" and "D" Companies advanced to close support of the K.O.S.B. At 1.15. pm "A" and "B" Companies moved forward to the railway HALTE North of BOUSSU. Some platoons of the SUFFOLK Regiment, (14th Brigade) under 2nd Lieut GEORGE joined and remained close to A and B.

23rd August. continued.

While the Brigadier was with the Battalion, news of Lieut PEPYS' death came, and Lieut DENISON was sent to take over the command of the Battalion machine guns. (about 2.30.pm.) Two British Aeroplanes coming over from the North were followed by German gun fire. The first aeroplanes seen in action. Written instructions for taking up a second position near WASMES, in case of a general retirement, were left by the Brigadier. Captain LEDGARD, (YORKSHIRE Regiment, attached) was sent back to reconnoitre roads leading to the new position "C" Company (Captain LUTHER) was ordered to reinforce the K.O.S.B. on the Canal bank, one platoon being in position by our own Machine gun section, which continued to do good service from time to time when good targets offered. Towards 6.0.pm Lieut-Colonel STEPHENSON, Commanding K.O.S.B's, requested O.Commanding K.O.Y.L.I. to take over the positions held by his Battalion on the Canal bank. This operation was completed by 7.0.pm. "C" and "D" Companies and Machine gun section occupying the Canal line, "B" Company (Major YATE) immediately in support, extended East of the Railway embankment, with "A" Company extended West of the embankment. By this time the 14th Brigade had retired, leaving only the Machine gun section of the E.SURREYS in position on the railway embankment The K.O.S.B. Battalion retired to the HALTE previously occupied by "A" and "B" (K.O.Y.L.I.).

The enemy were shelling the bridge head by the Canal lock, 300 yards East of the Railway bridge. The bridgehead was abandoned, an attempt to destroy the drawbridge which it covered, had met with no success. A second charge was being prepared by the R.E.Officer on the spot. Firing was ordered

23rd August. continued.

at intervals after it grew dark, to be taken up all along the Canal bank, in order to convey the impression that the defence of the Canal line was being maintained. The rifles were directed against the woods on the North bank, in which enemy might concentrate before attempting to rush the bridges. Up to this time there had been some casualties among the K.O.S.B's, and a few mwn of the K.O.Y.L.I. were hit. Targets offered by the enemy had been difficult, as the enemy were occupying the ditches and other cover, which concealed them almost entirely. It was only when a dense body advanced across the right front of our Machine gun section, in order to rush a bridge on this flank, that the Machine gun section opened fire. They did great execution, and their fire was so well maintained that the attackers retired again into the woods. The enemy were effectually stopped here for the rest of the day. It was while observing the result of this firing from a position on the Canal bank outside the Machine gun section, that Lieut PEPYS was shot through the head. After dark, German bugle calls were sounded all along the line, and died away, the distance Northwards. They appeared to be sounded to give the impression that they were retiring Northwards. Also, Refugees came in from the North, among them a Priest, who declared the enemy to be retiring Northwards.

No credence was placed in their reports, and it was judged that the enemy were moving Westwards to envelop our left flank. Gradually towards 10.0.pm. some Companies were withdrawn to the HALTE. The ~~Battalion~~ Adjutant Capt. ACKROYD rode in to Brigade Head-Quarters for orders. He brought back verbal orders from the Brigadier to retire to the second position. "C" Company remained to extricate

23rd August. continued.

our own Machine gun section, whose position it was difficult to reach, owing to the number of ditches to be crossed, and to come back without drawing the enemy's attention to the retirement, as rear guard. The enemy all the time was using star rockets to discover our dispositions. Neither the railway bridge nor the drawbridge had been badly damaged in our attempts to blow them up.

As a point of interest, it may be noted, that no Germans in this section crossed the Canal during the night, although they were in great numbers on the Northern bank, and their fires could be seen. A small party of the K.O.Y.L.I. under Sergeants MULLINS and WALKER who were accidentally left in the village by the Canal bank observed German ~~[illegible]~~ Patrols cross the Canal at day break followed by Infantry Column.

Following the K.O.S.B's, the K.O.Y.L.I. retired along the road towards DOUR, and then Eastwards towards WASMES.

Part of the ~~[illegible]~~ Battalion Transport with Captain LEDGARD, who was leading the way, became detached in the darkness owing to the fall of a transport horse in a cart, and consequent delay, and were temporarily lost to the Battalion, (~~[illegible]~~).

The Battalion was halted for two hours rest in a cornfield one and a half miles from WASMES, near LES PETITES FAILLIES.

"C" Company came in to bivouac, having left the Canal bank, finally, about midnight. The Machine gun section with them.

The Machine gun section brought Lieut PEPYS' body with them, having had no opportunity of burying him.

24th August. Monday.

Those who were wet through from wading across the dykes, found little rest during the two hours halt, but all buried themselve in the corn which had just been cut, and the sleepers were hard to awaken, and indeed to discover, in some cases, when the

Word

24th August. continued.

was passed round to fall in. At 4.0.am, when the dawn was showing, the Battalion was on its way into WASMES. It was difficult to get precise information about the new line. The CHESHIRE Battalion, (15th Brigade), was passed in LITTLE HORNU, nearer WASMES. Artillery positions were in course of preparation, and the men of the 15th Infantry Brigade were digging trenches for the incoming Brigades. The 2nd Bn K.O.Y.L.I. made a detour across the fields to avoid drawing the fire of the enemy, whose batteries were already opening fire further to the East. All night long, to the North and East, patches of the country had been lit up by the flames of burning villages, and it was obvious that the enemy were in close proximity. A halt was made in an open space under an avenue of trees on the outskirts of the town. Preparations for breakfast at once commenced. Lieut PEPYS' body was decently buried. Endeavours were made to gain touch with the Head-Quarters and the other Battalions of the 13th Brigade. The K.O.S.B's were found to be a few hundred yards further on. Lieut EGERTON, galloper to Brigadier-General CUTHBERT arrived, and indicated the position to be occupied by the K.O.Y.L.I.

[probably 9th (of 14th Bde)]

An advance was then made forward about a mile, a line of half dug trenches was struck, which connected on the left with trenches which the SHROPSHIRES were digging, and on the right were masked by a long line of railway buildings which presented a blank wall facing us. Beyond this again, Eastwards, were the W.RIDING Regiment, but their trenches could not be seen owing to the buildings in the corner of the town, which intervened. A party of this Battalion on a slag-heap

24th August. continued.

in advance of the railway buildings, was located.
Owing to the fact that the trenches that apparantly had been commenced for our occupation, were commanded by the slag-heaps to the immediate fronts N and E of them, "A" and "B" Companies of the K.O.Y.L.I. and the Machine gun section, were advanced across the branch railway line which crossed their front, and held in readiness for occupation of the line of slag-heaps should the enemy come on.
Major YATE, who Commanded these Companies, himself occupied a position of observation, with one platoon, (2nd Lieut HIBBERT'S). Near him was Major EUSTACE JONES, who, from this forward position, commanded his Howitzer battery, (52nd Battery R.F.A.), which was now in position in the line of the half dug trenches.
The other two Companies were in support South of the railway line, with Battalion Head-Quarters established on a slag-heap in line with the horses of the 52nd Battery. Communication was established by cyclist orderly with the 13th Brigade Head-Quarters, and all Companies, and the Machine gun section
The forward Companies of the K.O.Y.L.I. occupied their position from about 6.0.am. Immediately across their front and parrallel to it, some Companies of the W.KENT Regiment were entrenched about 400 yards forward. The ground between the slag-heaps and a village to the North-East was absolutely flat and intersected by low hedge-rows. The road to the village ran perpendicularly through the position, and the entrances to the village were some 2000 yards to our front. The enemy's troops were continually debouching ~~for~~ from the villag

24th August. continued.

but were always caught by the fire of the 52nd Battery, who made splendid practice. The bulk of the enemy's force seemed to move Southwards towards the position East of us, as no attack was developed immediate against our front, though forces of the enemy appeared to extend as if to attack, covered by their machine guns which occupied a line of cottages on the edge of the village. These cottages were shelled to pieces by the 52nd Battery, who followed with their fire, the enemy in their Southward advance, until the guns reached the limit of their traverse.

Our forward Companies never opened fire or gave away their position until the retirement commenced.

About 10.0.am. a preliminary order to prepare for retirement was received. The retirement was to be conducted in conjunction with the field Batteries, to whom the order was to be passed. After the 52nd Howitzer Battery had been withdrawn, "C" Company, K.O.Y.L.I. fell back to the Head-Quarter slag-heap, and took up a position to cover the retirement of the other Companies. Finally "B" Company actually came away at about mid-day. Positions were taken up by alternate Companies until the whole Battalion had passed the end of the road to BAVAI, by which we were to retire, the enemy infantry coming on very slowly, but pursuing vigorously with his artillery fire. In the meantime, the K.O.S.B's, who had been left by the Brigadier to help to cover the retirement, had been able to continue their march. A Company of the MANCHESTER Battn of the 14th Brigade, and our own "C" Company, who continued to hold the east of the slag-heap, which our Head-Quarter had previously occupied, came in for a heavy Artillery shelling

24th August. continued.

as they came away. A little delay again was caused while Major BALLARD's Battery of R.F.A. extricated itself under a fierce fire The K.O.Y.L.I. Battalion suffered a few casualties from the gun fire in the retirement.

The K.O.Y.L.I. now formed the rear guard, passing Southwards by the road to WARQUIGNIES and HOUDAIN. Near WARQUIGNIES a halt was made while our guns came into action to the North, and orders were shortly afterwards received to resume the march in column along the road. The road became much blocked and the marching slow, owing to the congestion, but HOUDAIN was reached in the evening, and directions received there on the bridge to proceed, skirting BAVAI, and to join the remainder of the 13th Brigade, who were found in bivouac, one and a half miles West of BAVAI. The Division was concentrated here. The 3rd Division was hard by.

A roll was called. Our casualties, (killed, wounded and missing) amounted to, One Officer and 27 N.C.O's and men only.

The Quarter-Master and ~~much of the 1st Line~~ part of the Battalion transport and personnel were absent. Emergency rations were opened. Men bedded down in freshly cut corn. The Battalion furnished one or two small picquets.

25th August. (Tuesday)

An early start was made at 3.0.am, on a long and exhausting march to LE CATEAU. BAVAI was skirted until the great main road leading South-West was struck. The rear guard to the Division was found by the Battalions of W.KENT Regiment and K.O.S.B's. The march led through the Northern edge of the forest of MORMAL. The enemy began to press during the morning, and slight rearguard actions took place, but the march of the column was not seriously interfered with.

25th August. continued.

Owing to the heavy casualties of the day before, the W.RIDING Battalion was this day marching with a strength of about 7 Officers and 400 men.

LE CATEAU was reached in the afternoon. Just before crossing the railway line outside the town, a halt had to be made to allow a force of 6 French Cavalry Regiments and a Cyclist Battalion to file across our front over the bridge.

We learnt from Headquarters at 1.p.m. of the arrival of the 4th Division, via ~~CALAIS~~ BOULOGNE, who were now occupying ground covering our Northern flank.*

A bivouac was ordered in the cornfield West of LE CATEAU, by the side of the road to REUMONT. The corn was freshly cut. We ~~[illegible]~~ had been joined ~~in the evening~~ on the march by our ~~[illegible]~~ Battalion "train" transport. Water had to be procured from a distance, food was issued at night. It rained heavily. At about 9.30.pm. our Company "A" was ordered out on outpost duty to occupy a line facing North-East, from the B of BREQUETIERE on the right, to the corner of the wood North of ARBRE on the left.

26th August. (Wednesday)

At 2.35.am. orders were received detailing arrangements for a renewed retirement. The order to stand to at 3.30.am was repeated. The orders specified the part to be played by the K.O.Y.L.I. in rear guard. It was to hold on, in conjunction with the K.O.S.B's on its left, to the position of trenches at present covered by our outpost Company, until 11.0.am, by which time the Divisional train would be clear. "If the situation permits" the rear guard was then to retire. From the time of arrival of these last orders, the Battalion had less than one hour to prepare. Supplies had to be distributed from the 1st line wagons which had arrived over night; new maps had to be got at, and the Battalion then had to go forward

* that a strongly entrenched position had been prepared for us in the neighbourhood of LE CATEAU, and that a large force of the French Army, rumoured as six Corps, were moving up to the East of us, against the left flank of the German advance.

25th August. continued.

in the dark, and take up a position not previously reconnoitred. "C" Company,(Captain LUTHER) was ordered to occupy the high ground overlooking the village of LE CATEAU, South of the BAVAI-REUMONT road, this was too extended a position for one Company to hold. North of the road, "D" Company (Major TREVOR) carried on the line parallel to the LE CATEAU-CAMBRAI road and West of it. North of "D" Company, the trenches between that Company and those to be occupied by the K.O.S.B's were allotted to "A" Company (Major HEATHCOTE), whose Company, already on outpost, had to be concentrated.

"B" Company, (Major YATE) were held in reserve and ordered to dig themselves in near the crest of the slope which overlooked the line of trenches. The trenches already dug, existed only North of the road. They were disconnected and sited in parallel straight lengths at intervals, to oppose the approaches from the East. The great road to CAMBRAI which ran along their front, was in some cases only about 500 yards distant. It formed a valuable covered approach for the enemy, who concentrated under the cover of its banks without exposing themselves. The road was edged with poplar trees.

Each of the three Companies in the firing line had to dispose of its half-companies in local support as best it could, using their field entrenching tools to throw up what cover they could in the time at disposal.

Before 6.0.am. however, dispositions were greatly changed. The position thinly occupied by "C" Company, obviously high ground of the utmost importance, was handed over for occupation by the 14th Brigade, with Lieut-Colonel STEVENS' Brigade of R/F/A, and the 52nd Howitzer Battery. "C" Company were brought across to

26th August, continued.

the North of the road and assigned a position generally in support of "A" Company. One platoon of "C" Company, under Lieut WILLIAMS, remained in the position of reserve, and continued to deepen the trenches already commenced, and now vacated, by "B" Company. Other trenches of the same system were occupied by the Battalion Signallers and Battalion Head-Quarters. In order to defilade the trenches now occupied by the MANCHESTER Battalion of the 14th Brigade, "B" Company was moved by the Brigadier-General to a new position facing South-East, in the ditches on either side of the REUMONT road. As the North side of the road was higher than the South, they formed two tiers of fire, and were able to produce considerable concentrated fire effect. A culvert under the road was used as a channel of communication between the two firing lines. They were fronting the village of LE CATEAU with a range of vision of about 600 yards to their front, and covering with their fire a low depression of the ground over which the enemy attacking from the East must advance to reach the trenches of the MANCHESTER Battalion. The left Platoon of "B" Company was detached about 60 yards, half each side of the road, under Lieut HIBBERT. Next to the left, the position of "D" Company, and of its supports, remained unaltered. That of "A" Company, again to their left, was a little extended, its left platoon being in close touch with the K.O.S.B's, and its right in touch with "D" Company, but the trenches being disconnected, inter-communication was impossible when once the action had commenced. The 122nd, 123rd and 124th Field Batteries had come into position almost in the line of our supports, the 124th on the right, immediately to the left rear of "B" Company.

26th August. continued.

A narrow sunk country road running East and West from the direction of LE CATEAU to the village of TROIS VILLES, marked the left of "B" Company, and divided this Company from the supports of "D" Company. Near the junction of this road with the big REUMONT road, the 124th Battery was in position, and the sunk road was full of horses and limbers etc:.

The net result of these alterations in the dispositions for the K.O.Y.L.I. was that the Head-Quarters, with "B" Company and one platoon of "C" Company were left South of the country road, while the whole of the rest of the Battalion was in position North of it, and a deep narrow road filled with Artillery etc: cut diagonally across the ground between the two halves of their position. To the right of the K.O.Y.L.I. the 14th Brigade was in full view, and close touch.

Before 6.0.am. an order was received in the Brigadier-General's handwriting as follows:- "Orders have now been changed. There" "will be no retirement for the fighting troops. Fill up your" "trenches as far as possible with water, food and ammunition". Later, Lieut-Colonel KINCAID-SMITH, of the II Army Corps Head-Quarters staff, rode up and repeated the order for "no retirement" This order was given to the signallers to be conveyed to all our Company Commanders, and Sergeant WILLINGTON, Signalling Sergeant, reported that this had been done. The Brigade Provost-Sergeant rode up to Battalion Head-Quarters to enquire for the exact position of the Battalion Commander, and to communicate the position of the Brigade Head-Quarters, (which was not connected by telephone) and the position of the Brigadier-General. He distinctly indicated the distant tree called "ARBRE" on the map, as the latter's position, and repeated this when questioned.

26th August, continued.

Messengers sent to this position returned, unable to find the Brigadier. However, communication by messenger with the Brigade official Head-Quarters was established, and an answer to a message asking that Lieut UNETT, Brigade Machine gun Officer, should be permitted to take command of the Battalion Machine guns for the day, was received in the affirmative, and Lieut UNETT arrived accordingly about 6.0.am and took over the Machine guns from Lieut DENISON, whose services were needed with his Company. Tea was distributed from the Battalion Cooker before 6.0.am, at the Battalion Head-Quarter position. Later, after the Companies had sent back their Company ammunition animals, which were now collected with the Battalion transport under the Quarter-Master near the place where the Battalion had bivouacked, the ammunition carts were brought up in turn, at a trot, and off-loaded alongside the Battalion Head-Quarter position. The boxes of ammunition were distributed to Companies by hand, by the signallers, as far as was found possible.

Some time after the action had commenced, Lieut UNETT moved his guns from the left of our position, where they had a poor field of fire, to the extreme right, taking up his position 50 yards South of the REUMONT road, on the right flank of "B" Company. Lieut RAWDON, Transport Officer, after bringing up spare ammunition and ordering the 1st line transport back, obtained permission to join his Company in the firing line.

The first shots in the day were fired before 6/am, by some German Cavalry, who were reconnoitring almost up to the lines. Not long after, enemy's guns came into action. One of the first guns ranging, threw a shell into our Regimental transport position.

26th August. continued.

The high ground now occupied by the SUFFOLK Battalion on our right, became the centre of an attack. The enemy poured a concentrated gun fire on our Batteries all along the line. The town of LE CATEAU appeared to be occupied by the enemy from the very first. His formations issued from the woods some miles East of LE CATEAU, and could be seen advancing in mass towards LE CATEAU. Also, three large bodies of troops appeared to disappear into the low ground South of the town, and to be pushing round the South of the position occupied by our Division.
The ridge held by the SUFFOLK Battalion was taken, and again reoccupied by the Battalion in counter attack. From the time that it was again occupied by the enemy. "B" Company and the right platoon of "D", (Lieut WYNNE) were constantly engaged. their fire was directed to prevent any further advance along the high ground, and coming from an unexpected quarter, was apparently very effective. Towards 3.0.pm, they witnessed an advance of dense masses of the enemy, of the strength of two Battalions, who swept over the crest, and down through turnip fields beneath the ridge. Allowing them to advance about 100 yards down the forward slope, they reserved their fire, and then all opened "Rapid". The losses of the enemy were numerous, and the whole mass moved back and disappeared again behind the ridge. Half an hour later, the enemy advanced again more cautiously, and it was then seen that he stretched far away to the South-West, enveloping our right. This constituted the third attack of the Germans in this quarter, which gained ground slowly, gradually concentrating their fire on "B" Company, until they almost enfiladed them from the South-west. The attack came from the direction of LE CATEAU. By Lieut HIBBERT's range card, the ridge was distant 600 yards, and fire

26th August. continued.

was opened on the massed attack at 500 yards distance.

Lieut WYTHE's platoon, ~~which~~ was the connecting link between "B" and "D" Companies, and was across the corner of the angle where their lines produced would meet, and was very much exposed to fire. ~~At the end of the battle, he had only 5 of the men with him who were not hit.~~

In order to support the attack on the ridge, the enemy, taking advantage of the cutting through which the CAMBRAI road ran, brought up a Battery of Machine guns and established them there. These guns were very troublesome all the day.

Lieut UNETT had called for volunteers to dig his guns into their position South of the road. The shrapnel fire was plastering the ground. Lance-Corporal KING and Private MITCHELL volunteered. When in position, he opened fire about 8.30.am on the enemy attempting to enfilade the SUFFOLK Regiment from a small round wood North-East of them, and threw back successive attacks along the ridge. Later, one gun was knocked out by a shell, ~~Corporal~~ Sergeant NUNN was wounded, and about 2.20.pm, when the 14th Brigade had retired and his right flank was open, he found it necessary to withdraw the remaining gun. The gun was carried into a trench of "B" Company's, and Lieut UNETT with the tripod came back to the Battalion Head-Quarter trench. The ground between the two was swept by a close and concentrated rifle fire by this time, and Lieut UNETT could not be permitted to attempt to bring the gun back to the place where his tripod was.

The gun was broken up before capture, in the trench.

At about 2.45.pm, Lieut UNETT was sent back to the Brigade Head-Quarters to explain the position of our exposed right flank, and to ask for assistance to recover the ground on our right.

26th August. continued.

The Brigade Head-Quarters had, however, been moved. He reported also that the W.KENT Battalion which had been entrenched in our rear about 100 yards back, was apparently moving back to a position further in rear.

The firing line of "D" Company, other than Lieut WYNNE's platoon, was heavily engaged to its front, and also with the enemy machine gun Battery on its right front. When casualties were heavy, Captain SIMPSON led a reinforcing party from the Company support line, under heavy fire, and got into the advanced trenches. He was himself wounded in getting there, Lieut NOEL was wounded about the same time. Further to the left, at about 11.30.am, Lieut BUTT, with number 11 platoon of "C" Company, reinforced the firing line, Sergeant PATTERSON (whose promotion to a commission dated from this day) bringing up the second half of the platoon. They continued to occupy this position until badly enfiladed from a position North of them, which was occupied by the enemy after the retirement of the K.O.S.B's. At about 3.30.pm, when the position was quite untenable, they attempted to retire to a position in rear. Lieut BUTT was now wounded, and Sergeant PATTERSON killed.

Some of "A" Company trenches were nearer the K.O.S.B. position. Sergeant MARCHANT was in the nearest, representing the extreme left. He was able, with the fire from his trench, to prevent the enemy from bringing machine guns up to their new position, but could not prevent the occupation of the high ground by ~~his~~ Infantry. His trench was unsupported, and he was unable to effect a retirement, and was eventually overrun by the enemy.

11.30.

At about 3.25.pm, Major HEATHCOTE and Captain LUTHER attempted to reinforce the "A" Company trenches, occupied up to this time by Captain GATACRE. The ground however, was swept by rifle fire,

26th August. continued. and only about a dozen men reached Captain GATACRE. Captain LUTHER was wounded. A great number of casualties occurred during this rush, including 2nd Lieut RITCHIE, who was killed. Captain GATACRE's trenches were overrun by the Germans some little time afterwards. Lieut DENISON was left mortally wounded in the head. Though blind he had continued to encourage his men in the trench, until he became insensible. He died in hospital at MONS some weeks later.

The line of resistance was rolled up from left to right.

"A" Company had come into action about 8.0.am, when "D" Company also opened fire. "B" Company, waiting for a dense target, opened fire generally some time after 11.0.am. By the time of capture, ammunition was completely exhausted in the front line trenches. Half the Battalion reserve of ammunition had been brought in before the action. After the action commenced it was impracticable to bring further carts up, or to distribute the ammunition by hand to Companies.

The enemy's Artillery bombardment, which had been directed in a great measure on our field guns, succeeded in silencing our guns an hour or so after mid-day. At about 1.0.pm there was a lull. The gun teams had been shot to pieces. One gun came out with a team of three horses. At about 1.30.pm the battle was renewed; the shelling and machine gun fire was directed on the Infantry trenches exclusively, the enemy infantry gradually gaining ground on the ridge West of LE CATEAU.

Some time before 3.0.pm, the whole of the ridge West of LE CATEAU was in the hands of the enemy.

By 3.10.pm, it was known to us that the W.KENT Regiment, the reserve Battalion of the Brigade, had been retired to a position in rear.

26th August. continued.

The higher ground occupied originally by the K.O.S.B's was in the occupation of the enemy. The position occupied by the K.O.Y.L.I. was now surrounded on three sides, but it was obvious that the Brigade as a whole, was occupying a position a little distance in rear. Retirement was out of the question, besides no order cancelling that of 6.0.am had been received by the K.O.Y.L.I.

A very heavy and accurate fire was directed on the trenches before the end. At about 4.20.pm the final rush came. In "B" Company, Major YATE ~~[illegible]~~ gave the order to meet it with a charge, but the number of men near him able to support it was so small, that his desperate call met with practically no response. Major YATE himself, with other Officers of his Company, was overpowered and disarmed. Lieut HIBBERT had been wounded.

The Battalion Head-Quarter trench was the last to go.

The single field gun which had been brought away, continued to fire down the road from a position in rear, while the enemy were overrunning the K.O.Y.L.I. trenches.

For some little time the Germans had been sounding our "Cease fire", and attempts were also made by them to call upon the K.O.Y.L.I. to surrender, but Major YATE, who commanded the firing line, refused to allow a flag to approach.

Besides 16 Officers, 320 rank and file were captured. (Wounded and unwounded).

On the 29th August, Major GRAY, R.I.F. was brought down the REUMONT road to LE CATEAU as a prisoner. Our dead were still unburied then, though there were burying parties at work over the fields. Major GRAY counted the dead on both sides of the road, chiefly in the "B" Company trenches alongside the road. He counted 62 bodies.

26th August, continued.

Sergeant CLARKE, whose commission was to date from the 26th August also, was killed in a "B" Company trench in the act of firing, by one of the last shots fired.

as to ~~The~~ the German ~~Division~~ troops with ~~which~~ whom we were immediately engaged, ~~included the [illegible] Regiments numbered 26 and 66. There were also soldiers of a HANOVER Regiment (with "GIBRALTAR" on their sleeves)~~, the following is quoted from LIEUT. WYNNE'S diary, from an entry made immediately after he had been taken prisoner :— "We were taken into the yard belonging to the remains of a farm at the cross-roads, and placed under a strong guard there. The troops that had captured our position and who now guarded us, belonged to four different regiments, the 26th, the 66th, the 72nd, and the 3rd Guards Regiment."

R C Bond Lt. Col.
2nd Battn. K.O.Y.L.I.

note: References are to the maps issued by the War Office for use on mobilization.

LE CATEAU.

No. 1. Original extension of 2/K.O.Y.L.I.

5 a.m. 26th August 1914.

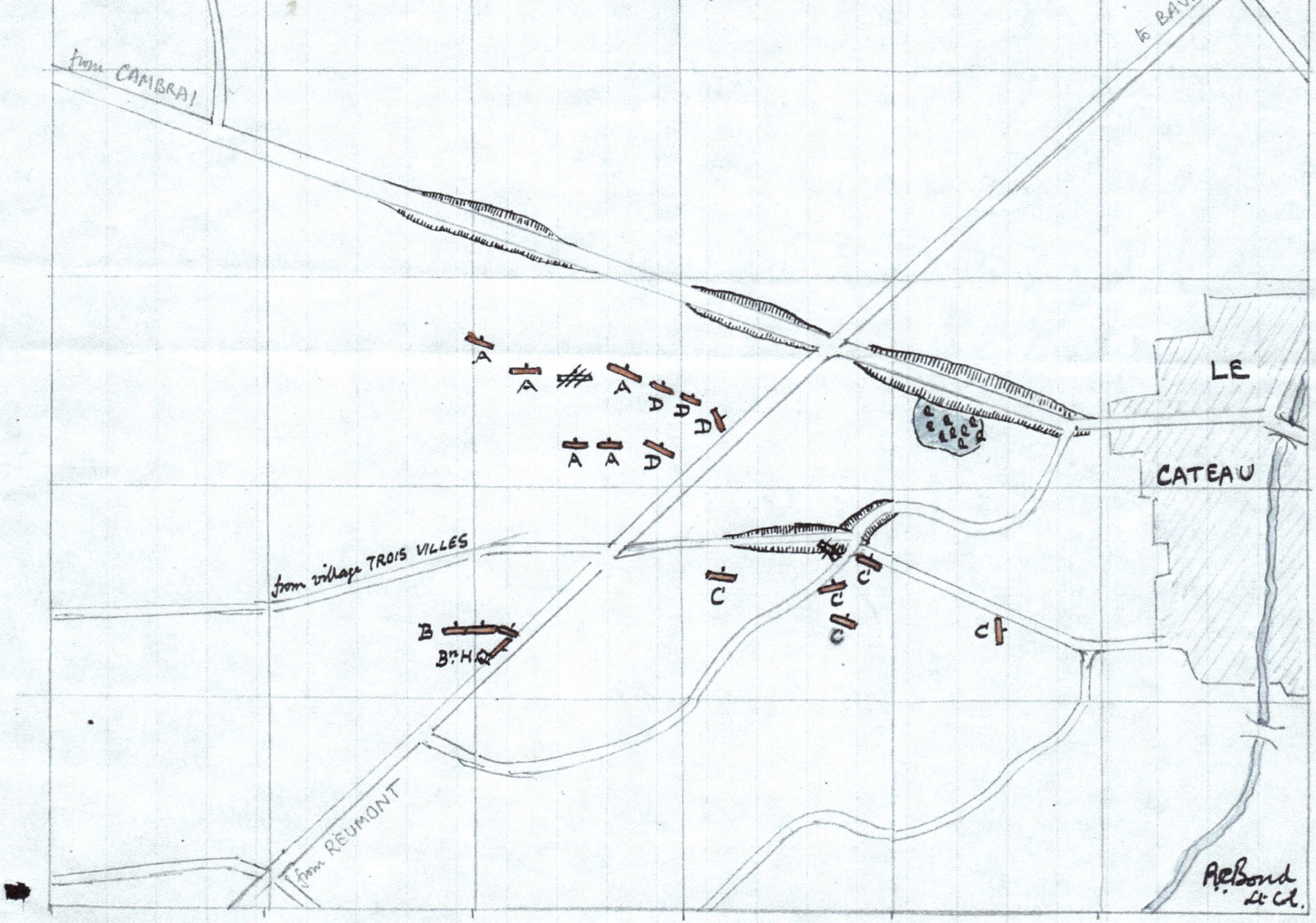

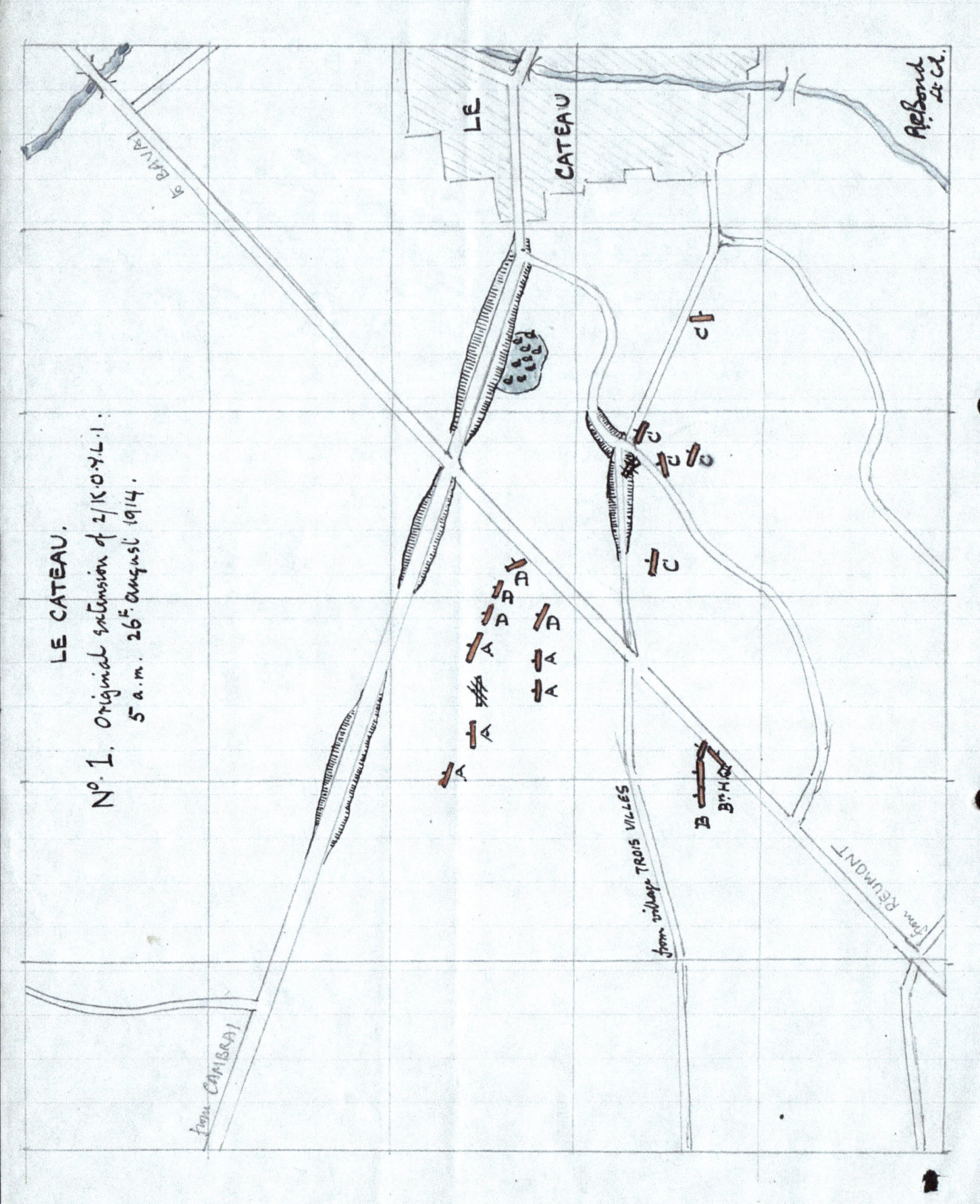

LE CATEAU.

No 2. Final position of 2/K.O.Y.L.I.

26 August 1914.

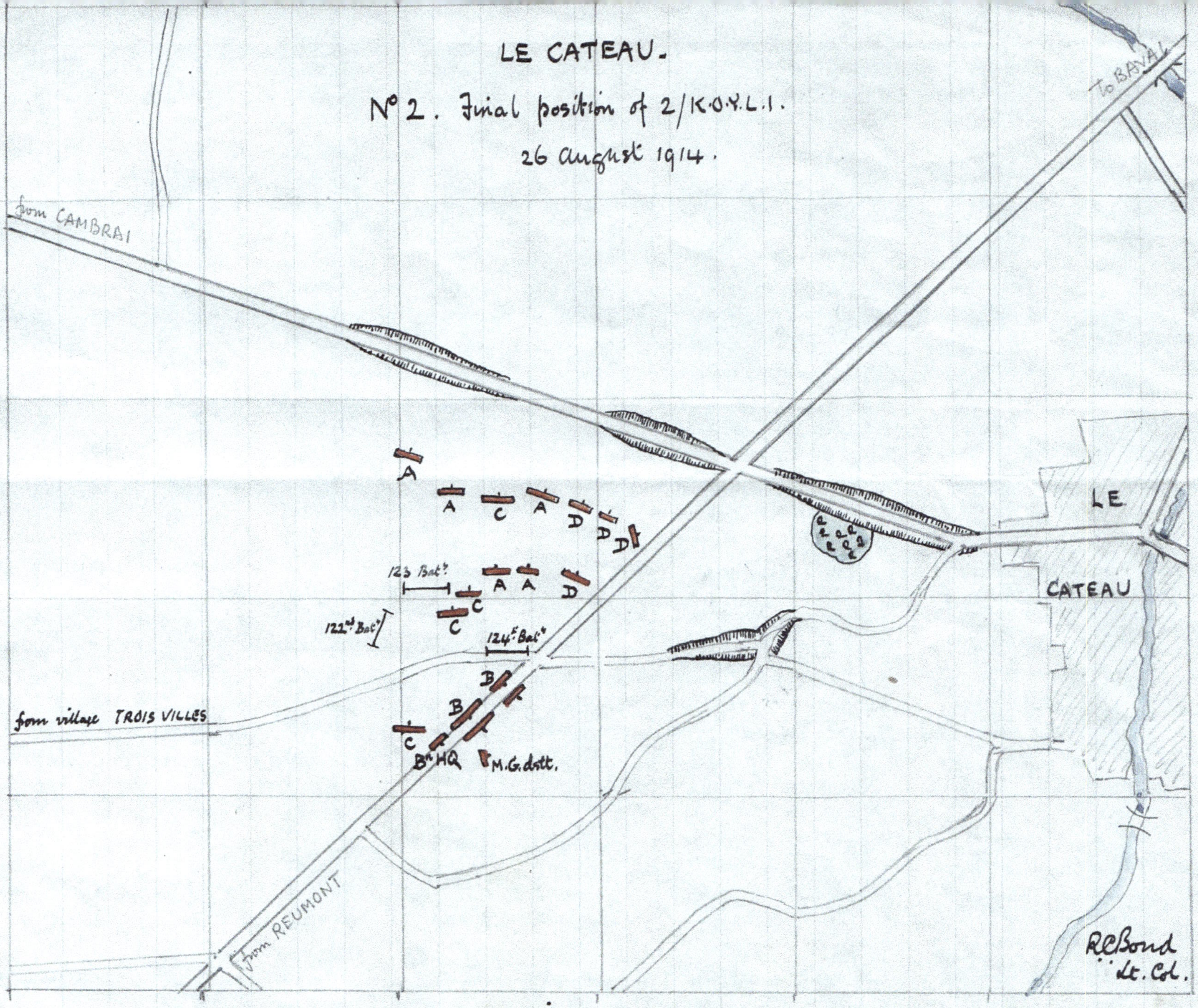

HISTORICAL SECTION,
COMMITTEE OF IMPERIAL DEFENCE
(MILITARY BRANCH),
PUBLIC RECORD OFFICE,
CHANCERY LANE,
E.C.

OFFICES OF THE WAR CABINET,
2, WHITEHALL GARDENS,
S.W.

June 1st. 1918

Dear Colonel Bond.

We are most grateful to you for the very full account of the battalion's share in the early part of the campaign: I wish we had something nearly as complete for other units. That is a fine thing about Denison — but no more than one would have expected.

What you tell us about August 23rd helps to explain a bit of the story which was specially obscure & the additional details of the rear-guard work on the 24th are most valuable. I suppose that B & C companies, who actually covered the retirement, did get a few chances of rifle-fire but your account confirms our impression that the Germans who had made the direct attack on the Fifth Division on Aug 23rd were distinctly chary about coming within effective rifle range next day. No doubt they were counting on the turning movement round by Elouges & further West — the stroke which Ballard's flank guard & de Lisle's Cavalry Brigade held off — & so may have pressed less vigorously, but even so it does look as if our musketry had inspired a wholesome respect.

There are a few points about Le Cateau which I should be very much

been quite so hardly treated — though hardly enough even so — but that they did get an opportunity of leaving their m[ark] on the Germans & that their end was like that of a battleship going down with flying colours.

With many thanks for your help.
Yours sincerely
C. T. Atkinson

obliged to have cleared up, though what you have already told us has made the story of the right flank far clearer than it was. The reason for B coy being posted as it was gave us entirely new light: we had read it as a reserve position not a fire position & thought the company was in ditches along the road as a local reserve. But can you tell us if the right platoons of B got any targets before the closing stages: the curved line X – X which we have marked on Sketch A is 1000x from those platoons, Y – Y being 2000x. Was it only the left platoons of B who opened fire at 11 A.M, as at that time the Suffolks' guns were still holding their own & I can't see any target for the right of B coy on the near side of the Selle

Can you say also what the ground was like in front of B coy: did it slope down rapidly to the S.E.? We have an account from the Manchesters of their advancing along the lines M – M which must have been straight across Yate's field of fire unless the section of the ground was such that they could cross his front unseen or right below his position

Sketch A shows the positions of the neighbouring units as marked by officers belonging to them: thus Col. H L James, the C.O. of the Manchesters, marked his battalion, Major R.M.G. Tulloch put in the R. West Kent, Major Tew who commanded that half-battalion of the East Surreys marked them & the Suffolks – the batteries

The placing of B coy on Sketch A differs from your sketch – we got it from Peebles of the Suffolks who had it, I think, from Yate.

were marked by officers of those units, six of the seven batteries by the Battery Commanders. Have you any comments on them from what you recollect? For example were the East Surreys quite as far forward. Tew was a little uncertain about the placing?

We gather that Wynne's platoon of D & Hibbert's of B must practically have swept the front of the left trenches of the Suffolks & that their fire was extremely effective in preventing the Germans closing with that battalion much earlier. The Suffolks say that most of their men never had a decent chance of using their rifles, as they had no field of fire, & one would have imagined that a frontal attack on them might have been made much earlier. Could you get Wynne to mark the direction in which he got his targets. The spot I have marked 2 is about 500x from him & 600x from Hibbert as far as I can make it. I wonder if that is it.

Wynne's identifications of the units against you are most useful but we are surprised to find the 3rd Guards among them, because the Corps that regiment belongs to was miles away fighting the French who had retired from Charleroi. Perhaps they were a machine gun detachment only. I wonder if he remembers if there were very many of them.

Our greatest difficulty in fitting in all the different accounts is that of reconciling times. It must be very hard indeed to keep any accurate record of times in action & one isn't surprised to find people in the same unit an hour different for the same event. For example the R.F.A. evidence is practically unanimous in putting the effort to get the guns away as <u>after</u> 1.30 pm & as covering a period of 30 to 45 minutes. Your account seems to put it a little earlier (p 19) – but we weren't quite clear about this.
The failure of any order for the retirement to reach your H.Q. is a very good illustration

of the difficulties of communications on a modern battle-field, especially in open warfare. We find the Royal West Kents got the order all right & one account from the East Surreys speaks of getting the order at 3 p.m. However, here comes in the divergent times question. We notice your right was open at 2.10 p.m., when the last machine-gun had to shift. That makes it quite clear that we must bring forward the moment at which the increasing pressure drove back the Manchesters & so enabled the Germans to envelope the Suffolks' right. Colonel James admitted that he wasn't too certain of his times, especially for the closing stages & the same applies to Major Tew, on the other hand the capture of the spur on which the Suffolks were, with such Manchesters & 93rd Highlanders as had reached them, seems pretty definitely fixed as 2.45 p.m. Majors Doughty & Peebles of the Suffolks, Col. Stevens of XV. R.F.A. & several others were all agreed on that. But it was then I suppose, when the Manchesters got pushed back, that the right of B company got their chance of "rapid" at Germans in mass formations.

There was one thing which we couldn't quite understand. The account in the War Diary we have received coupled with the fact that Major Trevor & Major Heathcote were among the few who weren't taken had made us imagine that the battalion was rolled up from right to left & that the few people who got away were from the left & owed their escape to the fine stand made by Yate's company who covered them. But is it possible that when you say the battalion was rolled up from left to right you are facing to B company's front against the Germans swarming up out of Le Cateau?

Yes. Left to right. It was the supports who got away

One thing more – we should be grateful for any fuller details of the German advance against the rest of D & against A – targets, formations, how near they got.

MG batteries to right front, chiefly, practically all day & German inf? never advanced beyond the road opposite D, but the cuttings were full of ... Batteries on CAMBRAI road obscured by ... up to 400x. German ... up a high gun in the BAVAI ... 900x ... direct on us.

This is a veritable inquisition, I fear, but I hope you will forgive my zeal for definite details. We have felt that the Suffolks had a very hard fate in getting done in without a fair chance of getting their own back: I am glad to think that the battalion to whose kindness I owe so much should not have

Gylisme & Noel fired on the Germans who appeared behind the ridge, but got no good targets.

Extract from letter

from Col. Bond

loss. PA! Le Cateau Col. Bond 2/K.O.Y.L.I.

Hotel Royal
Scheveningen
11 July 1918

13/5

Dear Atkinson

My affairs are much scattered in Holland, which fact must account for the delay in answering your last, of 1 June. I am forwarding you letters or statements from Hebbert and Reynolds which answer your questions fairly in detail. Also a letter of Wynne's.

As to the maps A and B which you sent me (and which I herewith am returning) I have made a slight alteration in the position of Wynne's platoon.

Rawdon's trench carried on almost to the road BAVAI-REUMONT. Wynne's left was about 100 yards from Rawdon's right. The position of B Company trenches was as I showed them on my sketch map i.e. all the Company were West of the Country road which ran to the village of 'Troisvilles'. Thus you will see that Trevor with his 'D' Co' support was in a position to fire to his right flank towards LE CATEAU without being masked by any portions of other Companies. Trevor moved Wynne forward at about 7.a.m. to get a better firing position for his platoon and cover some portion of the right flank, which as far as Trevor was concerned was left open, leaving him open, that is, ~~[illegible]~~ to enfilade fire from the direction of LE CATEAU. Wynne was at once under fire and could only effect what he calls 'rabbit-scrapings for lying-down cover': he occupied a line on the N.W. side of the road: he had 3/4 of his platoon with him, the other 1/4 being left with Trevor.

~~As to Targets:~~ As to the Germans on Aug. 24th being chary about coming on, I agree with what you say. It was remarkable that though we saw numerous infantry debouching from the villages to our front, no attack developed. Eustace Jones with his How: battery did remarkable service. He had his observation position from which he signalled his orders, right away in front of his guns on the slag heap by Yate's side: he was most cunningly concealed, and neither he nor Yate was discovered by the enemy. It was due to his battery (and others) that the enemy apparently could not develop their attack against this section of our position.

Yes, I think Wynne's & Holbrook's fire, and that of Unett's machine guns had a lot to do with preventing the Germans driving their attack home on the Suffolks: you see Reynolds also with the bulk of B Coy, was in a position to fire at times.

As to the identification of the 3rd Guards Corps, I cannot add anything myself, except that as far as I remember it was a young officer of this Corps who was placed in charge of us prisoners in Le Cateau on the second day after our capture. The G men who were guarding us belonged to the other Regiments, but this young officer wore a crown upon his shoulder-straps.

As to the times, I am quite prepared to hear that I am slightly early in my time when the effort to get the guns away was made, and I would accept 1.30 p.m as the time. I made my notes next day when a prisoner, and times like this had to be put in from memory. Some of my times were very distinctly printed on my memory, and I have felt from certain accounts of the retreat which I have read that my times would place certain events rather earlier than the times given and hitherto accepted. e.g. the 'order to retire' received by the W. Kents and E. Surreys, would I think have been received before 3 p.m. At any rate my flank was open at 2.20 pm. to some extent, when Unett had to shift with his machine-guns, and he and others drew a tremendous fire from the direction of LeCateau when they moved.

Our battalion was rolled up from left to right. The first trenches occupied by the Germans were those on the extreme left under the fire of the slightly higher ground which had originally been occupied by the right of the K.O.S.B.s : and so on, through Gatacre to Simpson, Noel and Rawdon : then to Wynne and on to Yate and B Coy : finally to the Batt: H.Q.

These trenches were the firing line plus Bn H.Q who were in a line with Yate; but who were masked by the position of the E. Surrey and Manchester Regt: up to the afternoon.

Galaen and Noel and the front line facing East were early in action, firing on the Germans who apparently held the LeCateau-Cambrai road, but they never got a good target, for the enemy simply contained them along this front. Rawdon who was further to the right was engaged chiefly with the machine gun battery to his right front practically all day. Directly to his front the trees along the Cambrai road obscured his view beyond a 400x limit. The Germans brought up a single gun on the high ground South of the road to BAVAI, which fired 'direct' on Rawdon's trenches at 900x: he had other infantry targets about this distance away on this slope.

I hope this has answered your questions satisfactorily. Fire off as many questions as you like: I will do my best to answer them.

Yours sincerely R C Bond

Rough copy of letter to Lt Bond - 105th

We are very glad indeed to have so full an account of the battalion's share in the beginning of the campaign. What you tell us about Aug 23rd & 24th is extremely valuable & helps to explain an obscure part of the situation and the additional details for the rear-guard work on the 24th are most helpful. I suppose that the companies (B & C) which actually covered the retirement got a few opportunities of rifle fire but your account confirms an impression that the Germans who had made the direct attack on the Fifth Division on the 23rd were distinctly chary about advancing within effective rifle range next day. No doubt they were counting on the turning move. went round by Elouges & Andregnies which Ballard's flank guard & de Lisle's Cavalry Brigade held off but it does look as if our musketry had inspired a wholesome respect.

Then about Le Cateau: the reason for B coy being posted as it was gave us an entirely new point, we had thought it was not in a fire position but in local reserve & but there might have been ditches along the road which gave it cover. But can you tell us if the right platoons of B coy got any targets before the closing stages: the curve X — X which we have marked is roughly 1000x from those platoons, Y - Y is 2000x. Can you also say if the ground sloped rapidly down from B coy's position to the S.E., because we have an account from the Manchesters of their advancing along the lines M — M which must been straight across Yate's field of fire unless the section of the ground was such that they could cross his front unseen.

The guns shown on sketch A were all marked for us by officers of those batteries, six batteries out of seven by their B.C.'s: the Suffolks were marked by their two senior officers, the Manchesters by their C.O. (Col. H.L. James), the East Surreys by Major Tew commanding that half battn, the R. West Kent by Major R.M.G. Tulloch. Have you any comments on them from what you recollect: for example were the East Surreys quite so far forward

We gather that Wynne's platoon of D coy & Hibbert's of B must have practically swept the part of the left trenches of Suffolks & that their fire was extremely effective in preventing the Germans closing with that battalion much earlier for the Suffolks say that most of their position didn't give them a decent chance of using their rifles & one would have expected that a frontal attack might have been driven home much earlier. I wonder if you would get Wynne to mark the direction in which he got his targets. His identifications of the unit opposed to you are most valuable but we are surprised to find Guards here: I wonder if he remembers if there were a lot of them or only a few. Perhaps they were machine-gunners, I believe the Guard Corps was many miles away opposed to the French at Charleroi

I suppose that it was only the left of B coy who opened fire at 11 AM. as at that time the Suffolks' guns were still holding their own & I can't see a target for the R of B this side of the ROSELLE

Our greatest difficulty in ~~reconciling~~ fitting one story in with another is the question of reconciling divergent times. Of course one can easily understand how hard it must be in action to keep any kind of record of hours, where there are no messages extant. ~~When you say "B coy generally speaks for some time of~~ For example ~~nearly~~ the R.F.A. evidence is practically unanimous in putting the effort to withdraw the guns <u>after</u> 1.30 p.m. & it seems to have ~~taken~~ gone on for nearly 45 minutes from first to last. We aren't quite clear if your account (p.19) doesn't place it a bit earlier.

The failure of any order for a retirement to reach your Head Quarters is a very good illustration of the great difficulty of communications on a modern battle-field (esp. open warfare), because we do find the order reaching the R.W. Kent & one account from the East Surreys speaks of getting the order at 3. p.m. Here again comes in the divergent time question we notice your right was ~~expose~~ open at 2.20 pm when the last machine-gun was withdrawn. However, Major Tow owned that his times were only very approximate. Similarly your account now makes it quite clear that we must bring forward the time at which the increasing German pressure ~~drive back~~ the Manchesters & so enabled ~~them~~ the Germans to envelope the Suffolks' right. [~~Col. James~~] It was, then, I suppose that B coy's right platoons got their chance of rapid fire at masses.

There is only one thing that we couldn't quite understand. Reading the account in the Diary & knowing that Major Trevor & Major Heathcote ~~to~~ were among the few who were not taken we had imagined that the rolling up was from R to L not as you tell us from L to R & that the few people ~~on the~~ were from the left & who got away owed their escape perhaps to the fire stand by Yate's company who covered ~~covering~~ them. But ~~do~~ when you say rolled up L to R are you facing to B coy's front against the Germans swarming up out of Le Cateau?

[Col. James like Major Tow wasn't too sure of the times in the later stages of the action – on the other hand Major Doughty & Peebles of the Suffolks, Col. Stevens of XV R.F.A. all put the capture of the spur on which the Suffolks were with such Manchesters & 93rd Highlanders as had reached them at 2.45] ~~an hour & a half before the Germans managed to~~

We have felt awfully sorry for the Suffolks because they got done in without a fair chance of getting a whack back. ~~This~~ I am glad to feel that a battalion to whom I owe so much should not ~~not~~ have been denied its chance of leaving its mark on the Germans but ~~even~~ that its end was that of a battleship going down with flying colours.

Hotel Pension Kieviet
Wassenaar
Holland

17 May 1918.

Dear Atkinson

I forward herewith a Copy of the Diary of the 2nd Batt^n for the period of the war up to 26 August 1914: I have attached two sketches to mark the position of the Batt^n on the 26 August (1) at 5 a.m. (2) final position. I have indicated the position of the guns of the three batteries 122, 123, & 124. I have purposely not indicated the position of any other of our troops, but should you require my idea of their positions, I can let you have them. Please let me know if you want any questions answered that I could assist in answering

Yours very sincerely

R C Bond

The 'British News' Offices.
Amsterdam.

July. 11.

13/5

Dear Colonel Bond.

I am extremely sorry to have been so long in answering your letter + returning the sketches. Rawlins, who owns the 'B.N.' has gone to England + insisted on my taking over the whole business during his absence of three or four weeks, which I rather reluctantly did: + have hardly had time to eat my meals since.

Capt. (Temp Lt) G.C. Wynne. 108 (V KOYLI)

Regarding Atkinson's questions — 1) I have marked on Map A the approx. position of my platoon + two lines drawn from it representing the general direction of my platoon fire from about 12.30 p.m, about when the Huns first crossed the Le Cateau–Cambrai road till 4.30 p.m (the lower line) after the Suffolks had been taken + the ridge was in ~~the~~ German hands. At about

4.30 p.m they advanced from that ridge almost at right angles to their original advance towards us on the BAVAI-REUMONT road: so that my fire was directed almost the whole time in the area between the two lines I have drawn in pencil on the map.

2) The 3rd Guards, or what I saw of them, arrived just after we had been taken & a certain number of them were detailed to look after us at the farm at the cross-roads (Pont des 4 Vaux on the sketch) & that evening were among the escort which took us (about 200 N.C.O.s & men) into the Le Cateau village. ~~[illegible]~~ At Mr Seydoux's house—when the officers were confined for a week—& a detachment (about fifteen I should say) of them took their turn with detachments of two other regiments (26th & 72nd I think) in guarding us. I don't think they were an M.G. detachment, though connected (say for certain.) of 3/. I have marked the position of my platoon on Map B.

If Atkinson, you mention, is the one who was attached to us at Aldershot will you please remember to him & wish him luck with his great work - which I'm sure he'll enjoy doing.

With kindest regards to Mrs Bond.

Yrs very sincerely

G. C. Wynne.

Note by Lt Col R. C. Bond

P.S. The time-table given by Wynne does not quite agree with the times given by me: it is possible that my time '4.20' given for the final rush is too early: this is the opinion of other officers captured with me, who think that '4.40' was nearer the mark. Still I have given the time as I originally wrote it for fear of exaggerating unintentionally the time that the battalion held out

RCBond

13th Brigade.

5th Division.

2nd BATTALION

KING'S OWN YORKSHIRE LIGHT INFANTRY

SEPTEMBER 1914.

2/K.O.Y.L.I.

Instructions regarding War Diaries and Intelligence Summaries are contained in F. S. Regs., Part II. and the Staff Manual respectively. Title pages will be prepared in manuscript.

WAR DIARY

or

~~INTELLIGENCE SUMMARY~~.

(Erase heading not required.)

Army Form C. 2118.

Hour, Date, Place		Summary of Events and Information	Remarks and references to Appendices
Tuesday 1st September ~~August~~ CREPY		Cavalry division of enemy reported to have been at COMPIEGNES yesterday. 2/Dublin & R.H. [illegible] on outposts during night 31st/1st with K.O.Y.L.I. and K.O.S.B. in support. Orders received at dawn that Maj TREVOR was to take over outpost line and command composed of 2 Battalions, 1 Bde Artillery and 5th Div Cyclists.	
	7 am	Orders received that march of force was cancelled, position of rearguard to be reinforced by whole of 13th Inf Bde under Gen CUTHBERT. K.O.Y.L.I. reinforced the right of the line from Pt 128 to LE PETIT MORMONT. A patrol of 60 or 70 of enemy's cavalry was reported to have been seen moving round the right. This was soon seen to be a feint and the left flank was finally shown to be the threatened flank. Firing became fairly brisk on this flank at times but the enemy brought up no guns and our own artillery did great execution on their advancing line. The attack was quickly repulsed. C Company assisted by a company of the 2/Dublins in wiping out 2 motor cars of the enemy which drove up with Staff officers and Machine Guns.	
	12 noon	The Brigade was ordered to continue the retirement and the evacuation of the position was carried out in perfect order, 2/K.O.Y.L.I. being told off to cover the retirement of remainder of the Brigade and hang on until the guns had retired to ridge South of CREPY. March continued through ORMOY and NANTEUIL to Billets in village of SILLY	Walker [illegible]
Wednesday 2nd September ~~August~~		Orders to move at 1 am ~~am~~ altered at 12.45 am to 4.15 am. March ordered to be continued via OGNES – VISSCAY – ST SOUPPLETS to CUISY which was reached about 11 am & Brigade went into Billets. Transport ordered to move at 6 pm to CHARNY.	Walker Lieut Adj
Thursday 3rd September ~~August~~	7.55 am	Marched via IVERNY – TAMBARDOU to COUILLY where orders were received for the Battalion to take up an outpost line from BOUTIGNY – QUINCY SEGY – COUILLY. Remaining Battalions billeted in COULOMMES.	Walker Lieut Adj
	5 pm	Orders received that portion of line QUINCY SEGY – COUILLY was to be taken over by 15th Inf Bde the 3rd Division connecting up on our right at B of BOUTIGNY. Whole Battalion in outpost line owing to length of line to be occupied. Orders received that outposts would be taken over by 2/Dublins at 10 am tomorrow.	
Friday 4th September		Piquet on MEAUX – QUINCY SEGY road ~~[illegible]~~ fired on by some Uhlans. The 2/Dublins did not take over the outposts until 12 noon soon after which intelligence was received ~~[illegible]~~ from 3rd Division that they were retiring their outpost line to the high ground North of VAUCOURTOIS. This left our right exposed & the Battalion was ordered to take up temporary outposts to fill the gap.	Walker Lieut Adj
	11.30 pm	Orders received to march via CRECY – VOULANGIS – FALMIERES to TOURNAN	
~~Friday~~ Saturday 5th September		Right ½ Bn marched at 12.15 am leaving the left ½ to follow on as they could not be got in from the outposts in time. Brigade arrived in bivouac in a field South of TOURNAN at 10.30 am. Reinforcements under Lieut W.G. CARRINGTON and 89 other ranks arrived. Strength of Bn 8 officers 512 other ranks.	Walker Lieut Adj

3K 04.1 I

Instructions regarding War Diaries and Intelligence Summaries are contained in F. S. Regs., Part II. and the Staff Manual respectively. Title pages will be prepared in manuscript.

WAR DIARY

or

~~INTELLIGENCE SUMMARY~~.

(Erase heading not required.)

Army Form C. 2118.

Hour, Date, Place	Summary of Events and Information	Remarks and references to Appendices
Sunday 6th September	The Great Retreat is finished at last, and orders received for Division to advance. Forwards again moving at 5.10 am to bivouac at VILLENEUVE. 2 Bns of 13th Inf Bde Advanced Guard. On arrival at VILLENEUVE orders were received to change direction in a [illegible] direction. 2/KOYLI finding Advanced Guard to a position covering DAMMARTIN and later changed to a position covering COURTRY. Information received that a general [illegible] was intended to be effected in a few days.	Watts Lt Col
Monday 7th September	Advance forwards continued to BOISSY via COULOMMIERS. ~~and~~ Bivouac in a field short of BOISSY. Heathcote rejoined this morning	Watts Lt Col. Recommendation ~~asked~~ for French Military Awards. See Appendix I
Tuesday 8th September	Orders received to engage the enemy wherever met with. Direction via ST GERMAIN – DOUE. Information received that enemy was blocked crossing the MARNE at LAFERTE. On arrival 1 mile short of MAUROY orders were received for 13th Inf Bde to attack position of enemy beyond ST CYR, 2/KOYLI on right and R W Kents on left in firing line, KOSB and 2/[illegible] cooperating with 14th Inf Bde moving direction towards ST OUEN on our right. During the advance the supports came under a heavy shell fire but owing to good extension only 4 casualties occurred wounded. Bn bivouacked in a field just S.W. of ROUGEVILLE. Enemy retired in some disorder in front of 14th Bde whose attack was delivered considerably behind ours. × Major Heathcote rejoined early in the day & commanded firing line. × 12 men rejoined Stragglers from LE CATEAU. 6 men went sick. Strength of Battalion 9 Officers 520 Rank & File.	5 casualties wounded Watts Lt Col
Wednesday 9th September	Orders to move early in morning and enemy was soon engaged. 14th Bde Advanced Guard. The Advanced Guard was hung up for a long time owing to one of the enemies batteries developing an enfilade fire from the left East of MERY, after we had crossed the MARNE at SAACY. We started towards PASSY where this check occurred. R.W.Kents and KOYLI were then ~~[illegible]~~ diverted and ordered to try and locate and capture this battery. We marched through COURCELLES to CAUMONT meeting a very large number of men and [illegible] of East Surrey and D.C.L.I. of 14th Bde who had apparently been caught in an ambush. R.W.Kents occupied high ground near MONTIGBARD, 2 Companies KOYLI formed strong [illegible] 500 yards along road to ST AUDE.	Watts Lt Col
Thursday 10th September	Orders received during the night that R.W.Kents and KOYLI were to occupy MONTREUIL by 4 am. KOYLI to be informed of hour of start by O.C. R.W.Kents and to conform with them. Owing to vagueness of orders sent to R.W.Kents, no orders reached us until 1.45 am, the R.W.Kents having started at [illegible]. The ground on ridge at MONTIGBARD was very thickly wooded and entirely unreconnoitred by us so that we lost our direction somewhat at the start. However, on debouching from a large wood we came straight on to the centre of R.W.Kents at CHAMOUST which was directly on our line of advance. We continued the advance without encountering the enemy, being in echelon on the left rear of West Kents to the N of MONTREUIL on which our left was directed.	

2/K.O.Y.L.I.

WAR DIARY

or

~~INTELLIGENCE SUMMARY.~~

(Erase heading not required.)

Army Form C. 2118.

Instructions regarding War Diaries and Intelligence Summaries are contained in F. S. Regs., Part II. and the Staff Manual respectively. Title pages will be prepared in manuscript.

Hour, Date, Place		Summary of Events and Information	Remarks and references to Appendices
Thursday 10th September (Cont)	5 am	Halted on line from point 400' East of M in MONTREUIL to the M.Q MONTREUIL.	
	8 am	Continued march via COULOMB - GONDALV - BAUMETZ to CHEZY where we went into bivouac.	Watts Lindsay
Friday 11th September		The Pursuit was continued via BILLY S/OURQ to HARTENNES where we went into billets. The last 2 hours of the march, there was pouring rain. The 13th Bde advanced guard with the Bn on head of main guard.	Watts Lindsay
Saturday 12th September		The pursuit was continued via DROIZY - CHACRISE - NAMPTEUIL - SERCHES to CIRY. On arrival ½ mile South of SERCHES the enemy were found to have taken up a very strong position to cover their retirement over the AISNE. It was found impossible to get on further than the X roads East of SERCHES. Artillery commenced to engage with enemy. Heavy fighting heard on our left from the direction of SOISSONS. Pouring rain all day. Bn went into close billets in SERCHES at nightfall.	Watts Lindsay
Sunday 13th September		R.W.Kent supported by K.O.S.B ordered to advance and seize the bridge over the AISNE at MISSY. Dukes + K.O.Y.L.I in support. On our arrival at CIRY it was reported that the enemy had taken up a very strong position on CHIVRES ridge and it was believed that their main force had turned round to defend it. It soon became evident that CIRY would very likely be subjected to shellfire, so the Battalion was moved to the sunken road at LES CARRIERES, ~~[illegible]~~ just below the crest of the ridge. The move was made only just in time as CIRY was shelled as the rear company left the village. The Transport had been ordered to march brigaded from SERCHES & had been caught in enfilade by enemy's artillery coming down road to CIRY. Owing to the prompt action of Lieut + Qr Master A.E. BENTHAM all the transport was turned round and got away with the exception of 1 ~~[illegible]~~ S.A.A cart smashed by a shell and 1 water cart overturned but subsequently recovered slightly damaged. Transport was subsequently got up to LES CARRIERES after dark. Lieut HAYES went sick and left with the supply wagons.	Watts Lindsay
Monday 14th September LES CARRIERES		R.W.Kent and K.O.S.B. were crossed river by ferry 100' below MISSY BRIDGE which had been destroyed by enemy. 2/K.O.Y.L.I. ordered to remain in their position.	
	1 pm	Enemy suddenly commenced to shell our ridge with high explosive and 2 men were killed and 5 wounded in a few minutes. Battery under cover below the ridge suffered rather heavily and apparently this battery was the enemy's objective.	Watts Lindsay

2K.OYLI

WAR DIARY

or

~~INTELLIGENCE SUMMARY~~.

(Erase heading not required.)

Army Form C. 2118.

Instructions regarding War Diaries and Intelligence Summaries are contained in F. S. Regs., Part II. and the Staff Manual respectively. Title pages will be prepared in manuscript.

Hour, Date, Place	Summary of Events and Information	Remarks and references to Appendices
Tuesday September 15th LES CARRIERES - LA GOBINNE Wood	Orders received last night to cross the river and concentrate with the Brigade on the other side before dawn. 2/K.O.Y.L.I. to follow 2/Dukes.	
1.30	Orders to move came. Bn moved off at 1.45 am. On arrival at MISSY BRIDGE it was found that the pontoons for crossing had not yet arrived. This left the Battalion in a very exposed position on the road with only about an hour before dawn. Maj Trevor ordered Bn to retire behind a row of trees about 400' behind the west end of the bridge. Enemy opened very heavy shell fire on the Battalion at dawn and owing to the exposed position and close ranks the losses were very heavy. B Coy which was in the most exposed position on the right of the line closed in on the centre and created more congestion. Horses and ammunition mules stampeded adding to confusion. The Battalion hastily entrenched at the front and rear edge of the trees and were soon under cover. In all the enemy gave us 3 bursts of fire, the last 2 not causing much damage. Nothing further happened during the day and we were ordered to hang on to our position for the night. Rifle fire opened during the night but no casualties. Rained all night and trenches became fearfully wet.	Casualties 53 killed & wounded. [signature]
Wednesday 16th September LA GOBINNE Wood. Dawn	Enemy opened with high explosive shell fire being very accurate. Only one trench was actually hit, 4 men being in it of whom 3 were blown to pieces and 1 was wounded. Enemy continued intermittent shell fire over our heads searching for our artillery. The following message was received from Lieut Gen Sir Charles Fergusson Comdg 5th Division:- SERCHES 15.9.14. My dear TREVOR, I am so dreadfully sorry that the regiment has suffered again. It is really a grief to me. I have been hoping to come and say a word to the regiment for a long time, but as you know, it has been hard to get an opportunity to do anything of the sort, but I shall do so at the first chance. Will you tell all ranks how very much their devotion and gallantry has been appreciated by me and by all who have watched them and tell them that I know they will not grudge the ~~[illegible]~~ sacrifice if they remember that it has helped the rest. I hope we shall soon hear good news of the general situation which I believe is very satisfactory indeed. I need not tell you and your men to cheer up and not be discouraged by these incidents, as I know their spirit is all right. We will [illegible] through in the end." Yours sincerely (Sd) Charles Fergusson. Major Trevor replies as follows:- My dear Sir Charles, All ranks of the 2nd K.O.Y.L.I. highly appreciate your kind letter received this morning which will be treasured in our Regimental records. Yours sincerely (Sd) H. E. Trevor 16.9.14	Casualties 3 killed 2 wounded. [signature]

(9 26 6) W257—976 100,000 4/12 H W V 79/3298

Instructions regarding War Diaries and Intelligence Summaries are contained in F. S. Regs., Part II. and the Staff Manual respectively. Title pages will be prepared in manuscript.

7 R. O. Y. L. I

WAR DIARY
or
~~INTELLIGENCE SUMMARY.~~
(Erase heading not required.)

Army Form C. 2118.

Hour, Date, Place	Summary of Events and Information	Remarks and references to Appendices
16th September 1914 (cont)	That night we retired to LA GOBINNE WOOD immediately in rear of us after dark where we found 9 new officers who had been posted to the Battalion:- Maj G.M. RENNY 3/KOYLI. CAPT R.H.S. STANTON late KOYLI Reserve of Officers. LIEUT T RICHMOND 3/KOYLI. 2nd Lieut C.E. WATKINS on 1st appointment 2/KOYLI. LIEUTS E.G. LAMB, B.E. HERVEY-BATHURST, and C.F. NUNNELY 3/ Northumberland Fusiliers. Lieutenants T.H. CLEMSON and E.N. BISHOP 3rd Dorsets.	[illegible]
Thursday 17th September LA GOBINNE Wood	Quiet all day	
Friday 18th September "	Quiet all day.	[illegible] Recommendations asked for [illegible] for British Awards. See Appendix I
Saturday 19th September "	Patrol of enemy reported at 7 pm to be this side of river. An officer patrol was at once sent out but found nothing.	[illegible]
Sunday 20th September "	Nothing happened all day.	[illegible]
Monday 21st September "	Nothing happened during day. Officers patrol reconnoitred river bank towards CONDE to see if reported footbridge existed. Footbridge non existent.	[illegible]
Tuesday 22nd September " 1 pm	Enemy's patrol of 10 managed to cross the river and passing by our right flank reached CIRY STATION. 2 picquets of ½ C Coy posted in copses on threatened flank to cover all ground up to CONDE Bridge. Very heavy firing heard in direction of VAILLY at nightfall.	[illegible]
Wednesday 23rd September " 8 am	Conference of C.O.s to visit the General and discuss plans for attacking enemy's position.	[illegible]
Thursday 24th September " 4 am	Orders received to change places with 2/Suffolks on N bank of river.	[illegible]
1 pm	C & D & C Coys crossed river to reconnoitre ~~ground~~ - position held by Suffolks. Coys to cross by ~~two~~ one at a time at 2 hours interval commencing at 8 pm.	[illegible]
Friday 25th September MISSY	No shelling all day & very little sniping. Companies settled down to their posts. A & B Coys taking right sector in reliefs and C & D the left sector. Work commenced on improving entrenchments. Defensive position determined on in consultation with Lieut SMYTH the Engineer Officer.	[illegible]
Saturday 26th September MISSY 8 pm	All quiet all day. Orders received in evening that French turning movement was progressing satisfactorily but that there was a possibility of Germans making a final effort to break through the centre. Troops enjoined to exercise constant and unremitting vigilance. Major J.R.G. TULLOCH arrived to take over command.	[illegible]

(9 26 6) W 257—976 100,000 4/12 H W V 79/3298

3/R.64.L9

Instructions regarding War Diaries and Intelligence Summaries are contained in F. S. Regs., Part II. and the Staff Manual respectively. Title pages will be prepared in manuscript.

WAR DIARY
or
~~INTELLIGENCE SUMMARY~~.
(Erase heading not required.)

Army Form C. 2118.

Hour, Date, Place	Summary of Events and Information.	Remarks and references to Appendices.
Sunday 27th September MISSY	Heavy shelling by enemy all day directed mostly on portion of defences near the church. Culminated about 5pm in terrific burst of shrapnel & [illegible]. Gen CUTHBERT came in the evening to discuss [illegible] of MISSY and the [illegible], delighted to find no casualties in 2 days [illegible] DORSETS and only 5 in KOSBs + 3 in R.B. [illegible]. Situation unchanged [illegible] vigilance [illegible] enjoined.	W.A.H.
Monday 28th September MISSY	Intermittent shelling throughout the day. No casualties. Generals Ferguson, CUTHBERT, + GLEICHEN came in evening to discuss feasibility of prolonging our line to the right to give more room for a jumping off place in the event of an advance. Patrol went out at night 1/2 [illegible] to reconnoitre the ground with the idea in view and also to endeavour to capture some prisoners with the object of finding out formation of enemy's troops in front. No result	W.A.H.
Tuesday 29th September MISSY	Intermittent shelling all day.	W.A.H.
Wednesday 30th September MISSY	Lieutenants [illegible] and [illegible] went out at 3am to CHATEAU near mill with intention of staying all day and endeavouring to capture some prisoners. They returned at 6 pm reporting that two Germans had approached the Chateau at 4pm and entered. 1 then turned into the cellar and the other into the hall with the result that one of our men got in between the two. They immediately fired and after that it was impossible to take them prisoner as they continued firing and using the bayonet. None of our men were touched and the 2 Germans were killed. A shoulder strap was taken and then the patrol retired via the river bank as a party of 28 of the enemy was approaching down the river. Nothing further happened during the day. Brig-General CUTHBERT came in the evening & very greatly [illegible] the Regiment on proceeding on leave [illegible]. All ranks feel they are losing a personal friend as well as a [illegible] Commander.	W.A.H. W.A.H. Farewell letter from B.G.C. see Appendix II

Appendix II

9/K.O.Y.L.I.

Instructions regarding War Diaries and Intelligence Summaries are contained in F. S. Regs., Part II. and the Staff Manual respectively. Title pages will be prepared in manuscript.

WAR DIARY

or

~~INTELLIGENCE SUMMARY.~~

(*Erase heading not required.*)

Army Form C. 2118.

Hour, Date, Place	Summary of Events and Information	Remarks and references to Appendices
	Farewell ~~letter~~ Order from Brigadier General G. Cuthbert CB Commanding 13th Infantry Brigade	
	In relinquishing the command of the Brigade I am so proud of, I want to say you one short word of goodbye, as owing to your being in the trenches I am unable to parade the Battalions and speak to you personally, as I should have liked to have done. I have known you now for 8 months, nearly all of which have been passed in the most severe campaign of modern times, and I have lived with you under all conditions, both of peace and war. Never has a Brigadier been better or more loyally served by all ranks than I have been by you; my orders fully and thoroughly carried out, my least wish anticipated and fulfilled. Your steadfastness and hardships, your gallantry and high courage under fire, and your unhesitating obedience and discipline, have been my constant delight and admiration; and your whole spirit, both Regimental and Brigade, could be equalled by none.	
	I have never been more proud to command you and in bidding you goodbye I wish you all health and success, added laurels, and a happy and speedy return home.	

13th Brigade.

5th Division.

2nd BATTALION

KING'S OWN YORKSHIRE LIGHT INFANTRY

OCTOBER 1914.

2/K.O.Y.L.I. 105th

Army Form C. 2118.

Instructions regarding War Diaries and Intelligence Summaries are contained in F. S. Regs., Part II. and the Staff Manual respectively. Title pages will be prepared in manuscript.

WAR DIARY

or

~~INTELLIGENCE SUMMARY.~~

(*Erase heading not required.*)

Hour, Date, Place	Summary of Events and Information	Remarks and references to Appendices
MISSY 1st October 14	All quiet during day. Relieved at 11 pm by 1st Bn Essex Regt. Marched at 11.40 pm & arrived in billets at VASSENY at 4 am	
VASSENY 2nd October 14	Marched at 6.40 pm into billets at VIOLAINE	
VIOLAINE 3rd October 14	Marched at 6.40 pm to billets ~~at~~ in HARTENNES.	
HARTENNES 4th October 14	Marched at 6.40 pm to billets in LARGNY 3 miles W of VILLERS COTTERET. whole column blocked for miles by troops marching in front, first 5 miles took 5 hours, arrived in billets 5.30 am	
LAGNY 5th October 14	Remained in billets.	
LAGNY 6th October 14	Marched at 6 pm to billets in FRESNOY	
FRESNOY 7th October 14	Marched at 7 am to VERBERIE, halted till 4 pm when Bn commenced to entrain for ABBEVILLE	
ABBEVILLE 8th October 14	Arrived and detrained at 9.15 am. Marched to Billets at DRUCAT. Marched off again at 6 pm to GUESCHART. Lieut Slingsby went sick.	
GUESCHART 9th October 14	Marched at 11.30 pm. Transport moving off at 8 pm with orders to go to DIEVAL. Brigade reached HARAVESNES about 2.30 am next morning.	
HARAVESNES 10th October 14	Remained Stationary till 2 pm when Bn moved off to a point short of VILLIEVRES to await Motor Busses. Batt all in busses by 4 pm arriving at VALHUON about 6 pm and billeted	
VALHUON 11th October 14	Marched at 8 am in Corps Reserve. On arrival at HESDIGNEUL information received that a gap existed between the French left and our Right. 13th Inf Bde ordered to fill it, went into billets at VAUDRICOURT and VERGUIN	
VANDRICOURT 12th October 14	Marched at 9.35 am. Still in Brigade Reserve. French attack on VERMELLES timed at 12 noon. 13th Bde advanced to fill gap between V of VERMELLES and the Railway. [Information received about 11.30 am that the Easterly movement of our Corps was progressing] 13th Inft Bde occupied line with KOSBs on left at Canal. D of W Regt in Centre. Royal West Kent Regt on right. Owing to French not attacking VERMELLES our right could not get on. KOYLI in reserve just N of G in ANNEQUIN.	
N of G in ANNEQUIN 13th October 14	5th Division ordered to attack all along the line at 5.30 am closely supported by artillery. Advance found impossible as French still not in possession of VERMELLES. About 3 pm Enemy commenced a strong counter attack against left of KOSBs and right of 15th Inf Bde. Reinforcements being asked for 'D' Coy were sent to reinforce the KOSBs, quickly followed by 'B' Coy going to hold the Railway Canal and road at PONT FIXE. KOSBs again asked for reinforcements and 'C' Coy was sent up to be held in Reserve. Dorsets suffered very heavily by being deceived by the Enemies apparent surrender. But one platoon of 'A' Coy was sent up past the firing line. 1 man slightly wounded of 'B' Coy. 1 man of 'A' Coy killed going into the firing line	

(9 26 6) W 257—976 100,000 4/12 H W V 3298

2/K.O.Y.L.I.

WAR DIARY
or
~~INTELLIGENCE SUMMARY.~~
(Erase heading not required.)

Army Form C. 2118.

Instructions regarding War Diaries and Intelligence Summaries are contained in F. S. Regs., Part II. and the Staff Manual respectively. Title pages will be prepared in manuscript.

Hour, Date, Place	Summary of Events and Information	Remarks and references to Appendices
H.Q. in ANNEQUIN 14 October 14	French stated early in morning that attack on VERMELLES would not be resumed but that day would be spent in improving the position. 13th Inf Bde ordered to do likewise. Enemy opened a burst of shrapnel near Bde Head Quarters, one Signaller wounded. Message received at 1-45 pm that French were to resume attack on VERMELLES at 2 pm supported by our Artillery fire and if substantial progress was made, the Brigade was to endeavour to co-operate. At 3 pm orders received that a French Territorial Battalion were to send representatives to take over Brigade position, and the relieving Battalion would move about 7 pm. About 3.30 pm orders received that a French Division was to make a determined attack on VERMELLES and to the North of VERMELLES. The attack to go right through our trenches. Our troops to co-operate by fire until French had passed through and then remain in trenches, as "point d'appui" until relieved by the Territorial Battalion. Meanwhile during whole day the trenches and village near PONT FIXE has been subjected to heavy shrapnel fire, & one platoon of B Company had to evacuate a house near the ridge for a short time as the position became untenable. B Company made some excellent practice at some German infantry trying to cross by a well aimed by reporting the movement to the Artillery - the whole movement was completely checked! Just before dusk a platoon of Germans came out from the edge of a wood & advanced in extended order towards the junction of our trenches and the K.O.S.B., these met the fire of "A" Coy trenches and a cross fire from the K.O.S.Bs and only about 5 got back. At dusk the Germans were heard passing orders and then gave a cheer which was answered by a terrific burst of fire from the K.O.S.Bs and "A" Coy. This attack of the Germans got to within about 30 yards of the K.O.S.B. trenches. One more attack was made about 7 pm which was equally unsuccessful and one imagines that the German losses must have been very heavy. Great difficulty was experienced in getting ammunition up to the firing line in places as the Germans were playing a Mac Gun on the road where the ammunition reserve was placed. Owing to the attack on VERMELLES by the French, it became very doubtful if the relief by the French Battn could take place much before dawn and as it turned out the trenches were not taken over until about 4 am. The Battn marched back into most comfortable billets at LE HAMEL, again being in Corps Reserve. __Casualties__ 4 Killed 12 Wounded 2 Missing	
LE HAMEL 15th October 14	Remained in billets. Major Kemp went sick. 2/Lieut A.H.P. Trengrouse with 5th reinforcement of 90 men arrived having been a month on the journey. Capt Lamb and Lieut Nunnerly left to join Northumberland Fusiliers.	

2/R. O. Y. L. I.

WAR DIARY

or

~~**INTELLIGENCE SUMMARY.**~~

(Erase heading not required.)

Army Form C. 2118.

Instructions regarding War Diaries and Intelligence Summaries are contained in F. S. Regs., Part II. and the Staff Manual respectively. Title pages will be prepared in manuscript.

Hour, Date, Place	Summary of Events and Information	Remarks and references to Appendices
LE HAMEL 16th October 1914	Orders received to move at 9 am to road junction S of the LE TOURET, met West Kents with whom we are in reserve to 3rd Division. K.O.S.B. in reserve to 5th Division D of W. & Dorsets attached 13th Brigade Corps Reserve. Went into billets at LE TOURET moved again at 2-30 pm to RICHBOURG L'AVOUE where the Battn billeted for the night. Major Trevor and 2/Lieut Carrington went sick. Strength of Battn 16 officers 839 R & F	
RICHBOURG L'AVOUE 17th Oct 14	Ordered to march at 9 am to L of PONT LOGY where we remained all day and went into billets at dusk. At 8-30 pm C.O. was ordered to go to 9th Bde Hd Qrs and orders were sent back that the Bn was to march at 2-15 am to relieve the R. Irish Rifles in the trenches in front of LANNOY.	
TRENCHES LANNOY 18th Oct 1914	Battalion on taking over from R Irish Rifles was informed that a general forward movement was to commence at 6-30 am with the Wiltshire Regiment on our Right and the Lincolns on the Left. As it turned out the Scots Fusiliers relieved the Lincolns about 6-30 am and were given the same objective as us viz the Chateau Wood. At 6-30 the Battn advanced with C + D Companies in the firing line and A + B in support. Neither Battalions on the flanks conformed and the line had to halt at 350 yards in front of the wood as they were subjected to fire from the edge of the wood and also enfilade fire from both flanks. A Coy went up in close support shortly followed by B Coy + Bn H.Qrs which established itself at the houses by the R L of LANNOY. The firing line entrenched themselves as best they could and the supports got good cover in a big trench which they improved. Considering the fire to which they were subjected the firing line did wonderfully well to get as far forward as they did, more especially as nothing on the flank got up level with them. Some splendid work was done in getting the wounded away from the firing line, especially by Sergt A Macdonald of D Coy who repeatedly went backwards from the firing line with wounded and returning with ammunition. Through the day we were in close touch with the 9th Bde group artillery. Lieut Helm R.A.M.C had his hands full through the day and in all some 70 wounded passed through his hands which he got away in the evening. About 5 pm we were informed that the Scots Fusiliers on our left were going to attack at dusk and try to get the FOURMES - ILLIES Road and C.O. informed 9th Bde that we would conform and passed the message on to the Wiltshire Regt. There was not time to get the orders to C Coy on the Left with results that the Scots Fusiliers advanced alone and almost immediately were given the order to retire. Unfortunately in doing so one Platoon lost direction and came back in our trenches who opened fire. The whole of the Scots Fus then retiring about to make back leaving our left absolutely exposed, and we had to refuse the left back to get touch with them. D Coy who had made another few hundred yards had also to [illegible]	
Casualties during the day 17 Killed 82 Wounded		

(9 26 6) W257—976 100,000 4/12 H W V
1250
3298

2/K.O.Y.L.I.

Army Form C. 2118.

Instructions regarding War Diaries and Intelligence Summaries are contained in F. S. Regs., Part II. and the Staff Manual respectively. Title pages will be prepared in manuscript.

WAR DIARY
or
~~INTELLIGENCE SUMMARY.~~
(Erase heading not required.)

Hour, Date, Place	Summary of Events and Information	Remarks and references to Appendices
TRENCHES LANNOY 19 October 1914	Nothing much happened all day. Orders received in evening the R Irish Rifles were to relieve us next morning.	
-do- 20 October 1914	Relieved by RIR at 4 am. Battalion went into billets at west edge of BOIS DE BIEZ. Orders arrived at night that we were to go back to 13th Bde the following morning.	
BOIS DE BIEZ 21st October 1914	Marched at 5 am to Hd Qrs 13th Infy Bde at FESTUBERT. Orders received at 4.30 pm to report to 14th Infy Bde at Cross Roads SW of NEUVE CHAPELLE. On arrival ordered to relieve DCLI at LORGIES by 4 am tomorrow.	
LORGIES 22nd October 1914	Marched at 2.30 am to the sound of a heavy night attack going on at our destination, luckily this died down shortly and the exchange of trenches was effected without casualties by 5 am. A C & D Coys came into the firing line with B in support this was arranged as B Coy had been sent for the previous night to do digging work on the new line of defence. The day opened at dawn by a terrific attack by the K O S B on our right who apparently attacked with the bayonet. Firing continued pretty hot through out the line especially on the right. On our front this soon died down and the remainder of the day was spent by the Battn in sitting under a steady and extremely accurate shell fire which continued throughout the day. Otherwise news came in about 11.30 am that Cheshires had been driven in on our right and the E Surrey had to retire their right slightly in consequence. At one time the situation appeared rather critical but this stage wore off and no further incident occurred till the evening when orders arrived for the evacuation of the position in favour of a line further back. 2/KOYLI were to leave at 12 mn and occupy line from Cross Roads SW of NEUVE CHAPELLE to L of RICHEBOURG L'AVOUE. Rear guard of 3 sections under Lieut Torrington to leave at 2 am. The evacuation was accomplished and the new line occupied by 4 am. A B C Coys firing line D Coy in support.	
TRENCHES RICHEBOURG L'AVOUE 23rd October 1914	Found necessary to send ½ D Coy to fill the gap between A & C Coys positions of enemy seen moving about 1000 yards from our line reconnoitring our new position	
-do- 24th October 1914	Nothing fresh reported in front enemy seen beginning to build up a line not very strongly held. Information received that a General Retreat was effected along whole line. Considerable movement observed towards our left flank along ~~the~~ ESTAIRE – LA BASSEE Road. Lieut Pollard RFA sent up to observe killed by shrapnel on arrival. Major J B G Tulloch went sick. Major C E Heathcote took over command of Battn. Heavy attack commenced towards evening, which was everywhere repulsed.	Tulloch went sick on 23

(9 26 6) W257—976 100,000 4/12 H W V

7/K.O.Y.L.I.

WAR DIARY
or
~~INTELLIGENCE SUMMARY.~~
(Erase heading not required.)

Army Form C. 2118.

Instructions regarding War Diaries and Intelligence Summaries are contained in F. S. Regs., Part II. and the Staff Manual respectively. Title pages will be prepared in manuscript.

Hour, Date, Place	Summary of Events and Information	Remarks and references to Appendices
TRENCHES RICHEBOURG L'AVOUE 25th October 1914	Hostile aircraft arrived early in day and directed enemy's heavy shell fire on our trenches. The result was a very severe bombardment which continued without intermission throughout the day. D Coy in support on the right suffered most heavily. Capt R.W.S. Stanton was wounded and owing to lightness of soil 2 men were buried alive and several more were only just got out in time. The men were considerably shaken but stuck splendidly to their posts and when the enemy made an advance about 3 pm our trenches wrought great havoc and successfully beat off the whole attack. Major Heathcote asked for reinforcement in case of emergencies and two Companies D.C.L.I. were sent up. They reinforced the front line during the night and repaired and improved the trenches which had been knocked about by shell fire. Sergt Wellington and Corpl Copley rendered very good work in bicycling along roads carrying messages to Bde H^d Qrs when shell fire was very hot. Two other Signal Orderlies were wounded. Unfortunately amongst the killed was 3 full Sergeants whom we could ill afford to spare. Total Casualties 17 killed 1 Offr. 25 men wounded. Reinforcement arrived with supplies consisting of Capt K.F.G. Carter 7/K.O.Y.L.I. 2/Lieut Shannon S.R. [struck through] S.L.I. 2/Lieut Corbally S.R. [struck through] S.L.I. 2/Lieut Carswell S.R. K.O.Y.L.I.	

2K.O.Y.L.I.

Instructions regarding War Diaries and Intelligence Summaries are contained in F. S. Regs., Part II. and the Staff Manual respectively. Title pages will be prepared in manuscript.

WAR DIARY

or

~~INTELLIGENCE~~ SUMMARY.

(Erase heading not required.)

Army Form C. 2118.

Hour, Date, Place	Summary of Events and Information	Remarks and references to Appendices
Richebourg d'avoué (near Bethune) ...nday Oct 26 - early morning	Very heavy shell firing on our trenches today from early morning. D Coy's trench was badly broken up for 40 yards. men were buried alive. Capt Stanton was wounded in the thigh by a piece of shell. The shelling consisted chiefly of so called "Jack Johnsons" the 738 lb lyddite shell. 17 men were killed and about 40 ~~[illegible]~~ wounded.	
10.30 pm	Capt H F G Carter arrived with draft of 149 men + 2Lt Carswell K O Y L I 3rd Res. 2Lt Shannon + Corballis P A S L I. The draft went straight & dug themselves into trenches.	
...esday Oct 27th	Heavy lyddite shell firing all day. Draft in reserve. Germans got through on left flank in small numbers. Our trenches were through some error evacuated. However on retiring on to main road all were rallied + trenches were retaken + most of the germans netted. Some 30 were killed while 6 or 10 were taken prisoners. ½ Draft remained in trenches. Lt Carswell killed Lt Watkins wounded. 2Lt Shannon sent home sick	
...ed. Oct 28 ...ursday - 29th	Still in trenches. Heavy shell firing + heavy casualties. Capt Richmond killed. A Coy's trenches got worst of shelling - though other coys had their share. Capt Carter's trench lost 9 killed and about 12 wounded. French artillery firing short accounted for a great many of these. - the same trench resisted a partial attack at 12 noon + enemy retired to trenches at 3pm 500 x away.	
...riday 30th	Quiet day until evening when enemy made strong attack which was repulsed. At ~~3.0~~ 3.0 am the Regt was relieved by 2nd Bn 39th Garwal Rifles + Bn retired to billet at Le Touret whence they moved at 2pm 31st for Merville where they arrived at 6pm. ~~At [illegible] orders were received~~ Our losses during the 9 days at Richebourg were roughly 300, 2 officers killed Carswell, Richmond. Officers wounded H B Ackhurst, Watkins Capt Stanton. Missing Lt Clemson. Sick Maj Tulloch, Lt Shannon	
Saturday 31st Oct. Sunday 1st Nov.	At 3.0 am the Regiment received orders to leave for Neuve Eglise at 6.30 am by motor bus to reinforce 2nd Cav Bde. At 10am we were told that Cavalry had had to evacuate their trenches E of Messines but that Cav Patrols still held the village. KOYLI + KOSB were ordered to attack + retake trenches. The trenches were not taken however as enemy's ~~[illegible]~~ machine guns occupied [illegible] of village + prevented any advance until our artillery should have destroyed the houses in which they were mounted.	On 31 Oct in attack N of MESSINES Capt Simpson & [illegible] were killed, Major Heathcote, Capt Stanton was wounded. This left Capt Carter, Lt Corballis only. Capt Smyth, Capt Hopson & two former [illegible] on night 31 Oct/1 Nov.

(9 26 6) W 257—976 100,000 4/12 H W V 79 3298

2. J.
[illegible]

2ND Bn. King's Own Yorkshire Light Infantry.

In France.

October to December 1914.

Copy of Letter dated "In France with 2nd Bn. K.O.Y.L.I. 16th October 1914" from 5216 Sergeant E. T. RICHARDS, 2nd Bn. KOYLI to Captain H. W. B. THORP, K.O.Y.L.I.

Friday, 16 October 1914.

Dear Sir,

The Battalion is still going strong in spite of casualties. More reinforcements joined yesterday which included several of our old Company at CRETE 1904, Section D men. Young Richards came up with the second lot of reinforcements and was in time to go with the battalion up to the AISNE. Our Brigade was the thin edge of the wedge between the Aisne river and the enemy. The Battalion was in support and had twelve killed the first morning we were there. I was scratched with a piece of brass on the ribs just below the right breast, nothing serious. I had a charmed life at LE CATEAU, but had to leave everything except my rifle; only ten of the company (B) from the trenches got back except a few who were wounded very early. I expect several of them are in German camps, as I have seen a photograph with a (B) Company Corporal on it. I am told that Major C. A. L. Yate has been shot while trying to escape.

We had thirty-eight hours in the trenches 12, 13 and 14th October 1914 and had a purely rifle and maxim fight from 6.30 p.m. 13th to about 3.30 a.m. 14th. We had three killed and four wounded. One German was acting the wounded Tommy and shouting out "Oh Sergeant Major I can not go any further". They also gave a poor imitation of our bugles on their trumpet, sounding the cease fire.

We did not see the result of the night fight as we were relieved by the Frenchmen at 4.0 A.M. and I occupied a feather bed at 9.0 A.M. the first since Dublin.

At present we are living in the Post-Master's house as X and have been for the last three hours and as it is getting dark we look like staying; if so, it means another feather bed to night as the Germans have not had time to burn everything.

Captain E.P.J.Stourton and Colonel R.C.Money are the only officers not with the Regiment that I have seen, though I have been very close to Capt. C.P.Deedes on two occasions.

Major T.B.G.Tulloch commands the Regiment at present and Captain Richmond, 3rd Bn. K.O.Y.L.I. commands "B" Company. Major G.M.Renny was in command of "B" but reported sick yesterday.

Portobello Barracks, Dublin has been cleared of all married families, and Mrs. Richards and daughter have gone to Hull.

We are getting excellent supplies of Tobacco and cigarettes thanks to the people at home and our rations are A.1. I could not feel sick if I tried since we arrived in France and I have no doubt you are the same.

I expect I shall figure in Army Orders for the Good Conduct Medal shortly; will you please let me know if you see it, Sir. A List of casualties to some you know. Private F.W.Eox (Crete) killed. Sergeant A.W.Palterson killed almost certain. Private

J.W.Christopher killed, I think he used to be your servant 1898-1899. Wounded C.Q.M.S. Whitworth, Sergt Patten (formerly Bugler), C.Q.M.S. Heslop, Sergt Barnes (1st K.O.Y.L.I.), Sergt C. Healey. I am the only Sergeant or Corporal left in the Company that marched out of Dublin with it.

Trusting you are well, I remain Sir,

Your obedient servant,

E. T. RICHARDS, Sergeant,

2nd K.O.Y.L.I.

NOTE.

On 16 October 1914 Sergeant E. T. Richards, 2nd K.O.Y.L.I. was probably at LE HAMEL as on night 14/15 October the 13th Infantry Brigade were relieved in the trenches by French Territorials and withdrew into Corps Reserve into billets at LE HAMEL, where a reinforcement of 94 men under 2nd Lieut. A.H.P.Errington joined 2nd K.O.Y.L.I.

No. 8216 Sergeant E. T. RICHARDS, "B" Company 2 Bn. K.O.Y.L.I. was killed in action either on 30/31 October 1914 in the fighting near RICHEBOURG L'AVOUE, or at MESSINES on 1st November 1914. He was awarded the silver medal for Long Service and Good Conduct by Army Order 412 October 1914.

Private E. T. Richards was soldier servant to Captain H.W.B. Thorp, 1904 to 1908 during which period he obtained a First Class Certificate of Education and was Best Shot of his company twice

1905 and 1907 and best shot in the Battalion (2nd Bn K.O.Y.L.I.) in 1907. He enlisted in 1896, served with 1st Bn. K.O.Y.L.I. in Beggars Bush Barracks, Dublin in 1898 where he married; and subsequently went out to the South African War 1899 in the Mounted Infantry. "Young Richards" is his younger brother who transferred from the Lincolnshire Regiment to "F" Company 2nd Bn. K.O.Y.L.I. at Hillsborough Barracks, Sheffield in 1906.

---

(2)

Copy of Letter dated "Headquarters Second Infantry Brigade, 1st Division, Expeditionary Force, Flanders, 16 November 1914" from Lieut. C.R.T.THORP, K.O.Y.L.I. Brigade Signal Officer 2nd Brigade, to Capt. H.W.B.THORP, K.O.Y.L.I.

Monday 16 November 1914.

Dear H.W.B.T.

The 2nd Bn. K.O.Y.L.I. were brought up into our line on 14th; they did well as usual but three officers, including A.B. Smyth, were missing when I went round near Harenthage at dawn yesterday (15 Nov.). Probably all killed. Withycombe is now in command of 105th with Carter as Adjutant. Fernyhough is our Divisional Ordnance Officer (1st Div.). I am fit but the weather is ---, showing and rain, trenches half full of water. I am doing temporary Staff Captain as well as Brigade Signal Officer 2nd Bde.

Yours,

C. R. T. THORP.

Copy of Letter from Lieut. C.R.T.THORP, K.O.Y.L.I., Brigade Signal Officer, Headquarters 2nd Infantry Brigade, 1st Division, dated in France 12 December 1914.

Saturday, 12 December 1914.

Dear H.W.B.T.

I met recently C. A. Heydeman of The Bays who was at Harrow with me. He was alongside 2nd K.O.Y.L.I. at Messines on 1st November and says our fellows did damned well; apparently he was one of the few officers who survived. He says he recommended Sergt. Marchant, 2nd K.O.Y.L.I. for the D.C.M. and is very anxious to know if he got it. He says that after all our officers had been knocked out, Marchant took command of the double company and brought them out of action and displayed considerable courage. You remember Marchant; he was corporal in "G" Coy, then Sergt in "F" Coy. at Hong Kong and before; an excellent fellow. We have great fun in the Brigade now practicing the Battalions in bomb throwing; the bombs are made out of bully beef tins etc; also rifle grenades which are quite good. They also carry a sort of Lacrosse-tennis racquet for warding off German bombs and throwing them back to the enemy's lines !, also several other new

Yours,

C. R. T. THORP.

NOTE.

No. 8310 Corporal C. T. MARCHANT, K.O.Y.L.I. was mentioned in despatches and awarded the Medal for Distinguished Conduct in the Field. London Gazette, 11 November 1914.

---

(4)

Copy of Letter dated "H.Q. 2nd Bn. K.O.Y.L.I. in France. 5th Division. Friday 1st January 1915" from Lieut. A.E.BENTHAM, Quartermaster 2nd Bn. K.O.Y.L.I. to Captain H.W.B.THORP,KOYLI.

Friday, 1st January 1915.

Dear Capt. Thorp.

I was very pleased to receive your two letters dated 24 and 26 December 1914. You will no doubt know that I came out to France with 2nd Bn. K.O.Y.L.I. at the beginning of the War; and I am sorry to say that I am the only Second Battalion officer at present left of those that embarked from Dublin in August.

We have 18 officers with us now and about 900 N.C.O's and men of whom 90% are Special Reserve. The officers are as follows, Lt.Colonel W.M.Withycombe, Capt. H.F.Day (acting Adjutant), Captains R.T.A.Ball-Acton, Buckle, Marten, Lieuts. Plumer, Gash, Childs, Slingsby, Williams, Singleton.

We are having an easy time just at present, as for twelve days an Infantry Brigade is holding a certain portion of a line - with two Battalions in the trenches for 48 or 72 hours and two Battalions in reserve in billets. This goes on for twelve days and then we go back for a six days rest as Divisional Reserve. We were lucky enough to get out for Christmas week and spent 23.12.14 to 29.12.14 at St Jean Cappel, and now we are at NEUVE EGLISE and take our tour of duty in the trenches near MESSINES.

Perhaps you know that it was at Messines that Major C. E. Heathcote was wounded and Capt. J.E.Simpson killed; also 5216 Sgt. E.T.Richards was, as far as information I can gather, wounded and owing to a retirement having to be made he never got back and the information regarding Richards in our Records here is "Wounded and Missing".

I was home on leave from 25.11.14 to 1.12.14 and went to Dublin during which time I visited Capt. E.P.T.Stourton at the St. Vincents Hospital; his hand is getting along as well as can be expected. I met him coming down in the ambulance when he and Major Heathcote were wounded at Messines; I was then at Neuve Eglise with the regimental transport. I have been doing both Quarter-Master and Transport Officer since 26 August 1914 when RAWDON was wounded; he was Transport Officer when we left Dublin but he went into the trenches at LE CATEAU with his company.

I shall be glad if Sergt T. March turns up as we have no Pioneer Sergeant at present; Sergt Harris was wounded 14th Sept, 1914 and has since died.

Yours sincerely,

A. E. BENTHAM.

---

(5)

An interesting coincidence.

Major Samuel Rice, 51st Light Infantry, writing during the Peninsular War, in later days often referred to as The Great War, from Headquarters, 51st Light Infantry at PENA MACOR dated 4 December 1811, writes :- "We have got papers down to 15 November 1811

Grand news was expected such as 'Northern Coalition', the old joke. I wish we could get those 'Russian Bears' on foot. Nothing can be done here but by something of the sort".

Lieut. C.R.T.THORP, 51st King's Own Yorkshire Light Infantry, writing during the European War of 1914, subsequently called The Great War, from Headquarters 2nd Infantry Brigade near ESSARS, north-east of BETHUNE, dated 27 December 1914 writes ;) "Good news from Russia to-day. I hope the 'Russian Steam Roller' will work. We want it".

13th Brigade.

5th Division.

2nd BATTALION

KING'S OWN YORKSHIRE LIGHT INFANTRY

NOVEMBER 1914.

2/K.O.Y.L.I

Army Form C. 2118.

Instructions regarding War Diaries and Intelligence Summaries are contained in F. S. Regs., Part II. and the Staff Manual respectively. Title pages will be prepared in manuscript.

WAR DIARY
or
~~INTELLIGENCE SUMMARY.~~

(Erase heading not required.)

Hour, Date, Place	Summary of Events and Information	Remarks and references to Appendices
Sunday 1st Nov. 2 pm.	By two pm the supporting companies + what remained of B + C Coys dug themselves in + prepared to hold line of ~~road~~ running N + S through Messine. Our casualties were very heavy – approximately 150 and 5 officers. Capt J.E. Simpson killed – Lt Errington wounded + missing. Maj Heathcote, Capt Stouton, Lt Chalker wounded. During the afternoon the Bays made some loopholes into back of a barn, they were however not watched + a party of Germans got in from the back after dark + firing through the loopholes killed 7 men + wounded Capt Stouton. Thus by 6 pm Capt Carter was left in charge of the Bn with 2 Lt Cornwallis, the only officer ~~[illegible]~~ left. About 9 pm reinforcements of 30 men + 3 officers arrived (Capt Hodgson 2nd Royal Fusiliers, Capt Smythe 2 K.O.Y.L.I, 2 Lt Sharpe PASLI) Capt Hodgson assumed command + Capt Carter the adjutancy. About 6 pm Capt Carter went over to OC London Scottish on left of KOYLI + arranged for London Scottish to fill in gap between KOYLI + Carbiniers which they had evacuated during afternoon.	
Monday 2nd Nov.	At 3.0 am 2nd Nov the Carbiniers were reported to have retired – at 6.30 am the London Scottish firing line retired, finding that its supports had retired earlier. This made the KOYLI untenable and left it enfiladed by 3 Bns of German Infty who advanced within 400x at 7.0 am. At 7 am KOYLI front trench retired on to supporting trench; but the Major i/c 18th Hussars on the left of our supporting trench seeing the pt was untenable ordered a retirement to the N side of the Wulverghem–Messine road. At 7.45 orders to retire came from HQrs 2nd Cav Brigade. The 18th Hussars + 4 DG however still held village + KOSB the S of MESSINE.	105
9.30 am	A report was at 9.30 am sent back by Col Burnett 18th Hussars to say that we had checked enemy all along new pn + could hold on: but unfortunately at this moment our own Howitzers opened fire on us + drove our line back causing some 100 casualties to our own troops. The MESSINES pn was evacuated + a fresh pn was occupied in trenches already dug E of Wulverden. KOYLI were relieved at 8 pm by 18th Hussars + retired to billet–	

3/K.O.Y.L.I

Instructions regarding War Diaries and Intelligence Summaries are contained in F. S. Regs., Part II. and the Staff Manual respectively. Title pages will be prepared in manuscript.

WAR DIARY
or
~~INTELLIGENCE SUMMARY.~~
(Erase heading not required.)

Army Form C. 2118.

Hour, Date, Place	Summary of Events and Information	Remarks and references to Appendices
Monday 2nd Nov. 8pm	at Neuve Eglise. KOYLI casualties amounted to 150 approximately no officers.	
Tuesday 3rd Nov	The following is copy of letter received by Bn from. 2nd Army HQ today 3 Nov. The Corps Commander has received a letter from Lieut General Allenby CB, commanding the Cav Corps an extract from which he publishes with much pride. HQrs Cavalry Corps 1st Nov. My dear Sir Horace. I must thank you for the help given to me during the past 48 hours by the Battalions you so kindly sent to our aid – KOSB, KOYLI, the Northumberland Fus" and the Lincolns. They arrived at a very critical time and their arrival saved the situation. I fear that they have suffered some loss but they fought brilliantly. I am deeply indebted to them and to Brigadier Gen Shaw. Yours Sincerely (Sd) EHH. Allenby". Z Rycroft Brig Gen. DA QMG 2 Army Corps.	Copy of letter received by Col Witheycombe from Maj ~~Mathew~~-Lannowe O.C. Bays. Arrow ~~Dear Colonel~~ ~~Dear~~ Colonel. On the 31st Oct in the action just North side of MESSINES your Regt (or part of it) advanced with us to reoccupy the ridge marked by the Ypres-Messines Road + together we held on to it up to + after the enemy's attack that evening. In my report as OC Bays I took the opportunity of bringing forward the names of Capt Carter who had become O-C of the Battalion owing to casualties & also that of Col Sergt Marchant. The line was broken at a point where there was rather a mix up of units + Sgt Marchant on his own initiative hurried back + brought back his men to reestablish the line. I take the liberty of bringing to your notice the excellent work (at a critical time) of Capt Carter + Col Sgt Marchant. Yrs Truly, Sd. Mathew Lannowe O C Bays (2 D Gs)
~~Thursday~~ Wednesday 4th Nov.	quiet day in Billets – following special order from Corps Commander was received today. To 2nd Corps. The Field Marshall commanding in chief has watched with the deepest admiration and solicitude the splendid stand made by the soldiers of his Majesty the King in their successful effort to maintain the forward position which they have won by their gallantry and steadfastness. He believes that no other army in the world would show such tenacity especially under the tremendous artillery fire directed against it. Its courage and endurance are beyond all praise. It is an honour to belong to such an army. The Field Marshall has to make one more call upon the troops. It is certainly only the question of a few days it may be only one of a few hours, before if they only stand strong support will come, the enemy will be driven back + in his retirement will suffer at their hands losses even greater than those which have befallen him under the terrible blows by which, especially during the last few days, he has been repulsed. The C in C feels sure that he does not make this call in vain — Jm. FRENCH. GHQ Ends	105

(9 26 6) W257—976 100,000 4/12 H W V 79/3298

2K.04.11

Instructions regarding War Diaries and Intelligence Summaries are contained in F. S. Regs., Part II. and the Staff Manual respectively. Title pages will be prepared in manuscript.

WAR DIARY
or
INTELLIGENCE SUMMARY.
(Erase heading not required.)

Army Form C. 2118.

Hour, Date, Place	Summary of Events and Information	Remarks and references to Appendices
Wed. 4th Nov.	Quiet day in Billets except that Bn had to leave billets suddenly at 3 pm till 6 pm and go into the fields behind NEUVE EGLISE owing to village being shelled.	[illegible]
~~Thurs~~ 5th Nov.	Orders to stand by at dawn. 8.0 am we were put under command of Genl Gough comdg 1st Cav Division. At 11.0 am moved to la Hutte in support of French attack on MESSINES. Returned to Billets 5 pm. Stood by 11.30 pm – 10 am + strengthened Picquets.	
Friday 6th Nov. Sat. 7th Nov.	Quiet day in billets. ~~Battalion at~~ Battalion stood to at 7.0 am on Saturday at 10 am moved to support Cavalry right flank near farm S of WULVERGEM B + A companies dug themselves in by bridge crossing river DOUVE 200 W of R. STERNBECK. At 5.30 pm after dark supporting companies and 30 men of R.W. Kent dug trench from Bridge to [illegible] thus connecting with IV Division line of Trenches on right flank. Battalion returned to Billets at 11.0 pm.	105
Wednesday ~~Sunday~~ 8th Nov. 9	Quiet day in Billets — [Voluntary church Parade in W Kent lines at 3.30 pm German aeroplane dropped 3 bombs on the parade unsuccessfully + missed.]	
Tu ~~Monday~~ 10th Nov. We ~~Tuesday~~ 11th Nov.	Quiet day in Billets 5.0 pm received orders to take over trenches from the French S of R. DOUVE. Very long business but eventually completed by 3.20 am. 2Lt Tomlinson + 4 men wounded by shrapnel while relieving. Trenches occupied [illegible] following companies D Coy Capt Hodgson, 2Lt [illegible] McCann 2Lt Snape. C Coy Capt Pyman (A Coy) ~~Capt~~ 2Lt Boardman. A Coy Capt Watson 2Lt Slingsby 2Lt Tomlinson. B Coy Capt Smyth 2Lt Grubb. 340 [illegible] relieved 900 French. French Soldiers brought back our wounded [illegible] allow our men to go into Trenches.	
Wed. 12 Nov	Some shelling [illegible] Received orders to be relieved by Devons. Adjutant [illegible] Devons at 4.30. [illegible] relief was not completed till 11.30 pm. Regt returned to Billets at NEUVE Eglise at 12.30 am.	
Thursday 13 ~~[illegible]~~ Nov	Halted for two hours near DICKEBUSCH + then [illegible] companies [illegible] through YPRES to open trenches ~~where~~ on Hooge Rd where Batt. [illegible]	
Friday 14th	Friday at 12.30 received orders to go to support [illegible] Fus in firing line. A [illegible] marched to Chateau on MENIN Road. At 7.0 pm the Chateau + stable which was in our firing line	

(9 26 6) W257—976 100,000 4/12 H W V 79/3298

2/K.O.Y.L.I.
WAR DIARY

~~Friday~~ Nov. 14. — was taken by the Germans. Capt Smyth with 50 picked men attacked the chateau and Stable at 7. pm. 2Lt Boardman with him. Lt Grubb was in near support with one platoon of D Coy. Remainder of D Coy in reserve. Attack was successful in retaking Chateau but Capt Smyth was missing afterwards. Lt Boardman wounded & 2Lt Grubb killed. Later Capt Hodgson evacuated Chateau which was retaken by Lt Cartaller & a platoon of D Coy. The Stable in front was still in hands of enemy. At 6.0 am 5th Fus's with aid of Field Gun brought up within 50 yards of Stable retook stable with very few casualties.

Sat. Nov. 15th — 2 Coys went in support of ~~Fifth Fusiliers~~ W. Riding at north of main Road. A Coy Capt Walsh, B Coy Lt Sharp by. Shelling all day. Lt Cartaller & 16 men of D Coy occupied trench in front of Chateau. & C Coy & MG occupied Reserve Trenches to our right front.

Nov. 15/16 — The same night we were ordered to relieve Lincolns in firing line, but owing to nonarrival of Bays this was only half completed.

Nov. 16 — Heavy shelling most of the day & in evening we took over remainder of firing line then held by Lincolns. C.O moved his HQ to pt 200" behind trenches.

Nov 17th — Very heavy day of shell fire & Capt Tymans Coy - C Coy - were shelled out of trench in front of farm. Men retired too far & were brought up with the Supports into firing line again by adjutant & C.O. under MG fire which accounted for 6 casualties. At dusk evacuated trench was reoccupied

105

2 K.O.Y.L.I.
WAR DIARY

Nov. 18th	Shelling with High Explosive & bombs started at 8.0 am & continued most of the day. Capt Pyman & 6 men were buried alive in their trench in front of farm which had to be again evacuated. Casualties occurred all along the line from shell fire & Capt Carter the adjutant was wounded in the hand while in HQ Dug out with CO. The dug out was nearly blown to bits & both CO & Adj had narrow escape. At 6 pm 5th Fusiliers relieved us & Bn returned to billets on Ypres-Menin road at 8 pm. Casualties during these five days were 13 killed 45 wounded 26 missing as well as Capt Smyth missing, 2Lt Grubb killed, 2Lt Boardman, Capt Pyman, Capt Carter wounded.
Nov. 19th	At 4.30 Bn moved out of Billets to relieve Lincolns who were in local reserve under 3rd Cav Bde. During the last 2 days the two following messages were received — "Gen Smith Dorrien wires "I am very proud of the grand reputation the 3rd & 5th Div have been earning during the desperate fighting under the 1st Corps." also The 4th Fus & KOYLI. The Corps Commander congratulates 9th Bde on the successful night's work" from 3rd Div. (ref to night of Nov 11th)
Nov 20th	The Battn remained in Local Reserve under 3rd Cavalry Bde until 10.45 pm. When it was relieved by the French & marched to LOCRE to Billets arriving at 2 am.
Nov 21st	In Billets at LOCRE. Capt M.F. Day with Draft of 193 NCOs & Men joined Battn at LOCRE.

K.04.LI

Army Form C. 2118.

Instructions regarding War Diaries and Intelligence Summaries are contained in F. S. Regs., Part II. and the Staff Manual respectively. Title pages will be prepared in manuscript.

WAR DIARY
or
~~INTELLIGENCE SUMMARY.~~

(Erase heading not required.)

Hour, Date, Place	Summary of Events and Information	Remarks and references to Appendices
LOCRE Nov 22nd — " — 23rd — " — 24th — " — 25th	In Billets at LOCRE. — do —	
— " — Nov 26th	Quiet Day in Billets at LOCRE. Capt Yates. 2 Lieut Plumer and Draft of 100 Rank and File joined the Battalion.	
LOCRE to NEUVE EGLISE. Nov 27th	[At 12 noon the Battn was drawn up & addressed in most complimentary terms by Sir J. French.] At 3 P.m. the Battn marched to NEUVE EGLISE & then through WULVERGHEM to a line of trenches 1½ miles East of this village with our right resting on RIVER DOUVE. The Battn relieved the Suffolk Regt in these Trenches.	105
Trenches Nov 28th	In the Trenches. The Battn H.Qrs farm heavily shelled between 7.45 and 9 am & partially demolished. Artillery Duel at intervals throughout the day & usual sniping on both sides, otherwise nothing of note to record. One man wounded. Our Trenches and those of the Enemy 150 yards apart.	
Trenches Nov 29th	In the Trenches. Desultory shell fire all day. Snipers active by day & night in bright moonlight. The 9th Queen Victoria Rifles joined us in our trenches, relieving some of our men.	
Trenches Nov 30th	In the Trenches. At 3½ ~~pm~~ our right trench was severely shelled with High Explosives & Mortar Bombs. Trench blown in badly in places. Only 2 Casualties.	

13th Brigade.

5th Division.

2nd BATTALION

KING'S OWN YORKSHIRE LIGHT INFANTRY

DECEMBER 1914.

WAR DIARY
or
INTELLIGENCE SUMMARY.

Army Form C. 2118.

Instructions regarding War Diaries and Intelligence Summaries are contained in F. S. Regs. Part II.

Place	Date	Summary of Events and Information	Remarks
Trenches	Decr 1st	In Trenches East of WULVERGHEM – Our artillery shelled the German trenches opposite our position & did great damage and silenced their Bomb Thrower which had annoyed us on the previous day –	
	Decr 1st (continued)	Draft of 5 officers and 190 Rank and File joined the Battalion – Officers – Capt Ball Acton – Lieuts Leather (19th Yorks Regt) 2/Lieuts Gash Hadow (19th) and Lee (19th) –	[initials]
Trenches –	Decr 2nd	In Trenches E of WULVERGHEM – all quiet bar usual desultory shell fire and sniping – one man killed –	[initials]
Trenches	Decr 3rd	In trenches East of WULVERGHEM – Nothing of note occurred – one man wounded	[initials]
Trenches to St Jans Cappell	Decr 4th	Relieved in trenches by 2/D.C.L.I. at 9 P.M. – at 10.30 P.M. the Battn marched to St JANS CAPPEL where we arrived at 1 a.m. & went into Billets.	[initials]
Billets	× Decr 5th	In Billets at St Jans Cappel.	[initials]
Billets	Decr 6th	In Billets at St Jans Cappel – Draft of 3 officers and 66 Rank & File joined the Battalion – Officers 2/Lt Williams, 2/Lt Hunter and 2/Lt Singleton –	[initials]
Billets	Decr 7th	In Billets at St Jans Cappel acting as Corps Reserve –	[initials]
—"—	Decr 8th		
—"—	Decr 9th		
Trenches East of LINDENHOEK	Decr 10th	Battn marched from St Jans Cappel at 2 P.M. via DRANOUTRE and LINDENHOEK into the trenches East of LINDENHOEK on the slopes of Hill 75 (Ref [illegible] sheet 3) where we relieved the Dorset Regt – the trenches were in many places waist deep in water owing to recent rains & 4 men got so badly stuck in the mud that it took 4 hours to get them out [illegible]	[initials]

(9 26 6) W 257—976 100,000 4/12 H W V 79/3298

Instructions regarding War Diaries and Intelligence Summaries are contained in F. S. Regs., Part II. and the Staff Manual respectively. Title pages will be prepared in manuscript.

WAR DIARY
or
INTELLIGENCE SUMMARY.
(Erase heading not required.)

Army Form C. 2118.

Hour, Date, Place	Summary of Events and Information	Remarks and references to Appendices
Trenches – Decr 11th	In trenches East of LINDENHOEK – The trenches here are very close to the Enemy's line – Only 50 yards apart in places – We occupy what used to be the German line of fire trenches, & they occupy, as fire trenches, what used to be their supports – Usual sniping by Day & Night & Desultory shell fire.	[illegible]
Trenches Decr 12th —"— 13th	In trenches East of LINDENHOEK – Draft of 95 R&F joined Battn	[illegible]
LINDENHOEK – Decr 14th	Relieved at 6 pm by K.O.S.B. & retired into Billets at LINDENHOEK –	[illegible]
Near LINDENHOEK – Decr 15th	Active offensive operations against WYTSCHAETE commenced by French 16th Corps & British 2nd Corps – (3rd & 5th Div). The Battn occupied entrenched position round Farm ¼ Mile East of LINDENHOEK just S of LINDENHOEK – WYTSCHAETE ROAD where it remained all day in Reserve, & withdrew into LINDENHOEK after Dark.	
Nr LINDENHOEK Decr 16th	Re occupied same trenches as on 15th & remained in Reserve. Some progress reported by 3rd Div towards WYTSCHAETE – Heavy Bombardment of WYTSCHAETE by our Artillery – German reply only slight – Our trenches shelled with Shrapnel but only 2 men hit slightly after Dark Battn withdrew to DRANOUTRE our place being taken by K.O.S.B. – No further progress made against WYTSCHAETE where the advance of both French 16th Corps & our 3rd Division was held up by strength of German Position –	[illegible]
Dranoutre Decr 17th	In DRANOUTRE – Offensive operations against WYTSCHAETE discontinued.	[illegible]

W 257—976 100,000 1/12 H W V 79 3298

Instructions regarding War Diaries and Intelligence Summaries are contained in F. S. Regs., Part II. and the Staff Manual respectively. Title pages will be prepared in manuscript.

WAR DIARY
or
INTELLIGENCE SUMMARY.
(Erase heading not required.)

Army Form C. 2118.

Hour, Date, Place	Summary of Events and Information	Remarks and references to Appendices
DRANOUTRE. Decr 18th	At DRANOUTRE.	
Trenches. Decr 19th	Marched from DRANOUTRE at 3 30 P.M. and relieved 9th Q.V. Rifles in the same trenches East of LINDENHOEK that the Battn occupied on 11th & 13th. Casualties during period 10th to 19th Decr 1914 5 Killed 11 Wounded 4 Missing. These Casualties were nearly all due to the enterprise of German Snipers.	RD
Trenches Decr 20th	In Trenches East of LINDENHOEK.	
— " — Decr 21st	" Our Centre trench shelled by enemy one casualty. Bombarded enemies advanced trench on our left with Trench Mortar and Rifle Grenades with good results.	RD
LINDENHOEK. Decr 22nd	Relieved in trenches by 9th Rifles at 6 P.M. & withdrew to LINDENHOEK for the night.	
[St Jan]s CAPPEL. Decr 23rd	Marched from LINDENHOEK at 7 am. [to Temporary Billets at LE RAVETSBERG. Continued the march at 3 P.M.] to ST JANS CAPPEL where the Battn went into Billets as Corps Reserve. Casualties 20th to 23rd Decr 1914 6 Killed & 11 Wounded. All due to Snipers & in different trenches. During the 3 days in these trenches we lost 80 odd men from swollen feet as a result of standing for 48 Hours knee deep in water & mud.	RD
St JANS CAPPEL Decr 24th	In Billets at ST JANS CAPPEL.	RD

(S.26 6) W 257—976 100,000 4/12 H W V 79/3298

Army Form C. 2118.

Instructions regarding War Diaries and Intelligence Summaries are contained in F. S. Regs., Part II. and the Staff Manual respectively. Title pages will be prepared in manuscript.

WAR DIARY
or
INTELLIGENCE SUMMARY.
(Erase heading not required.)

Hour, Date, Place		Summary of Events and Information	Remarks and references to Appendices
St Jans Cappel.	25th Decr – Xmas Day –	Hard frosty morning. Battn rested in Billets at ST JANS CAPPEL. In the afternoon a Football Six aside Competition was held & was won by A Company. After this the Officers played the Sergeants. A Draft of 92 Rank and File under Command of Captain Martin joined the Battalion.	
St Jans Cappel –	26th Decr, 27th Decr, 28th Decr	In Billets at ST Jans Cappel.	
To Trenches on RIVER DOUVE	29th Decr	Battn marched from St JANS CAPPEL at 12 Noon & Halted for 1½ Hours at NEUVE EGLISE marching again at 4.30 P.m. to WULVERGHEM & thence to the Trenches N of RIVER DOUVE along the STIVER BECK. Where we relieved the Norfolk Regt. Capt Buckle and 2/Lt Childs joined the Battalion at NEUVE EGLISE.	105
Trenches.	30th Decr	In Trenches. Our right trench shelled with High explosives at about 12 noon. Trench badly damaged in places. Casualties 3 men Killed and 3 wounded.	
Trenches.	31st Decr	Quiet Day – No Casualties. Relieved by 9th Q.V. Rifles & returned to Billets at NEUVE EGLISE – Where Battn remained in Support.	

(9 26 6) W257–976 100,000 4/12 H W V 79/3298

13th Brigade.

5th Division.

2nd BATTALION

KING'S OWN YORKSHIRE LIGHT INFANTRY

JANUARY 1915.

Instructions regarding War Diaries and Intelligence Summaries are contained in F. S. Regs., Part II. and the Staff Manual respectively. Title pages will be prepared in manuscript.

WAR DIARY
or
INTELLIGENCE SUMMARY.
(Erase heading not required.)

Army Form C. 2118.

105

Hour, Date, Place	Summary of Events and Information	Remarks and references to Appendices
at NEUVE EGLISE 1st Jany 1915	In Billets at NEUVE EGLISE.	
2nd January, 3rd Jany	In Billets at NEUVE EGLISE.	
4th –"–	Lieut. G H Kent & 2 Lieut T. Upton joined the Battn.	
5th –"–	Enemy shelled NEUVE EGLISE at 1 P.M. & 1 shell fell in Street just below our Billets & killed 9 men of the R. Rifles, 3 K.O.S.B., 1 K.O.Y.L.I. & local Padre & wounded about 25 more men.	
6th –"– Neuve EGLISE to Trenches in Sector B.	Marched at 5 P.M. to WULVERGHEM – thence to Sector B where we relieved the West Riding Regt. – very wet night. Inspected by Genl. Sir C Ferguson at 12 Noon who addressed the Battn. on taking over command of the 2nd Army Corps.	
In Trenches in Sector B. 7th Jany	Very heavy Rain & strong wind all day. The Douve overflowed its Banks & flooded out several trenches & cut off Battn. H.Q. from the firing line. Casualties 1 Killed & 6 wounded.	
Trenches – 8th –"–	Trenches heavily shelled most of the day. 4 Casualties –	
To Neuve EGLISE 9th –"–	Relieved by West Kent Regt. & marched to NEUVE EGLISE. No Casualties – Relief completed at 9 P.M.	
To BAILLEUL. 10th –"–	Marched from NEUVE EGLISE at 1.45 P.M. via DRANOUTRE to BAILLEUL & went into Divisional Reserve there.	
BAILLEUL. 11th –"–, 12th –"–, 13th –"–, 14th –"–, 15th –"–	In Divisional Reserve at Bailleul –	
To DRANOUTRE. 16th –"–	Marched at 12 Noon to DRANOUTRE. – 2/Lt J H Oldham 3rd D.C.L.I. joined the Battn.	

(9 26 6) W 257—976 100,000 4/12 H W V 79 3298

Instructions regarding War Diaries and Intelligence Summaries are contained in F. S. Regs., Part II. and the Staff Manual respectively. Title pages will be prepared in manuscript.

WAR DIARY or INTELLIGENCE SUMMARY.

(Erase heading not required.)

Army Form C. 2118.

Hour, Date, Place		Summary of Events and Information	Remarks and references to Appendices
at DRANOUTRE	17th Jany	at DRANOUTRE in Brigade Reserve.	
DRANOUTRE to Trenches in Sector D.	18th — " —	Marched at 4 P.M. & relieved K.O.S.B.s in Sector D – Trenches East of LINDERHOEK. 2nd Lt P.B. Rohan and 2nd Lt J. Rodgers joined the Batt. on promotion from the Irish Guards.	
Trenches in Sector D.	19th — " —	In trenches in Sector D. Very little shelling but Snipers very active. Trenches only 40 yards from Enemy's in places & Parapets & Traverses rendered very unsafe by washing away. Casualties 0.	
— " —	20th — " —	Snipers active as usual. Good work done by Corpl FINNEY & Pte Moore who patrolled by night through the German Barbed wire up to their trenches & gained useful information. Pte Moore captured or shot. Cpl FINNEY returned in safety. Casualties 5 killed & 3 wounded.	
To DRANOUTRE	21st — " —	Relieved at 7 P.M. by K.O.S.B.s & marched into Brigade Reserve at DRANOUTRE.	
DRANOUTRE.	22nd — " —	At DRANOUTRE. News received that 1st Batt. were at PATERSTEENE.	
To Trenches in Sector D.	23rd — " —	Paraded at 4 P.M. & marched via WULVERGHEM to Trenches in Sector D where we relieved K.O.S.B.s. Capts Mallinson & Stanley & Lieut Collis Browne all of 1st K.O.Y.L.I. attached for instruction in Trench work. Capt T.A. Ball acting wounded.	

Instructions regarding War Diaries and Intelligence Summaries are contained in F. S. Regs., Part II. and the Staff Manual respectively. Title pages will be prepared in manuscript.

WAR DIARY
or
INTELLIGENCE SUMMARY.
(*Erase heading not required.*)

Army Form C. 2118.

Hour, Date, Place		Summary of Events and Information	Remarks and references to Appendices
Trenches to BAILLEUL.	24th Jany	Quiet Day in trenches barring usual Sniping 3 men Killed + 3 wounded all by Snipers – Relieved at 7 P.M. by Cheshire Regt + marched into Divisional Reserve at BAILLEUL.	[illegible]
Bailleul –"–	25th Jany	At Bailleul. At midnight Battn received orders to hold itself in readiness to move at 15 minutes notice owing to reported concentration of enemy between MENIN and LILLE.	[illegible]
Bailleul.	26th	At Bailleul – Standing to all day ready to move.	[illegible]
–"–	27th	At Bailleul.	[illegible]
–"–	28th	At Bailleul. Draft of 1 officer + 98 men (Capt E [illegible]) joined the Battalion.	[illegible]
–"–	29th	At Bailleul. Battn marched towards OUTERSTEENE at 10.30 am to meet the 1st Battn which formed part of 28th Division + which had just arrived in France. The Two Battns formed up in a field facing each other + piled arms + fell out – after 2 hours meeting they each returned to their respective Billets.	[illegible]
–"–	Jany 30th	At Bailleul. Draft of 1 Officer (Lt Wilson) + 72 men joined the Battn.	[illegible]
–"–	Jany 31st	At Bailleul – Capt Marten [illegible]	[illegible]

13th Bde.
5th Div.
ATTACHED TO 28th DIV from 19.2.15

2nd K. O. Y. L. I.

FEBRUARY

1 9 1 5

Army Form C. 2118.

Instructions regarding War Diaries and Intelligence Summaries are contained in F. S. Regs., Part II. and the Staff Manual respectively. Title pages will be prepared in manuscript.

WAR DIARY
or
INTELLIGENCE SUMMARY.
(Erase heading not required.)

105 Th.

Place	Date	Summary of Events and Information	Remarks and references to Appendices
Bailleul to Trenches.	Feby 1st	Bailleul to Trenches in Sector D. Marched at 3 P.m. Via NEUVE EGLISE & WULVERGHEM & relieved 1st Norfolks in Trenches.	
Trenches.	" 2nd	In Trenches in Sector D. Artillery Duel all day.	
"	" 3rd	Moved to LINDENHOEK in Brigade Support. after relief by K.O.S.B.s.	
"	" 4th	Moved to DRANOUTRE as Brigade reserve. after relief by Duke of Wellington's Regt.	
"	" 5th	Dranoutre to Trenches in Sector D. & relieved K.O.S.B.	
"	" 6th	In Trenches in Sector D. very little shelling.	
"	" 7th	Moved to LINDENHOEK. Relieved by K.O.S.B.s & R.W.Kents. Lieut Plumer killed by a sniper.	
"	" 8th	Moved to LINDENHOEK in Brigade Support.	
"	" 9th	DRANOUTRE to BAILLEUL into Army Reserve Draft of 1 Officer & 34 men (2/Lt Chubb) joined the Battn at Bailleul.	
Bailleul	" 10th		
"	" 11th	at BAILLEUL.	
"	12th		
"	13th		
"	14th		
"	15th		

(9 26 6) W257—976 100,000 4/12 H.&.V. 79 3298

Instructions regarding War Diaries and Intelligence Summaries are contained in F. S. Regs., Part II. and the Staff Manual respectively. Title pages will be prepared in manuscript.

WAR DIARY
or
INTELLIGENCE SUMMARY.
(Erase heading not required.)

Army Form C. 2118.

Hour, Date, Place	Summary of Events and Information	Remarks and references to Appendices
At Bailleul Feby 16th	At Bailleul – Draft of 89 R+F joined the Battn. –	
—"— 17th	Battn. should have returned to Trenches E of LINDENHOEK but orders came to cancel this move owing to activity of Enemy S.E. of YPRES + 13th Brigade was ordered to stand by ready to move to YPRES –	
—"— —"— 18th	Still standing by at Bailleul –	
—"— to OUDERDOM. —"— 19th	13th Brigade marched from BAILLEUL via LA CLYTTE to OUDERDOM to relieve one Brigade of 28 Division who were holding the line, with indifferent success, S.E. of YPRES near St ELOI.	105
Trenches near VERBRANDEN MOLEN – —"— 20th	Marched from OUDERDAM at 6 P.M. via VLAMERTINGHE through YPRES + relieved 4th Kings Own (83rd Infy Bde) in the Support Trenches at BLAAUWEPOORT Farm near VERBRANDEN MOLEN – the 4th Kings Own had had a bad day of it having lost one complete Company in an attempt to retake No 32 Trench which had been lost that day –	
Trenches near VERBRANDEN MOLEN. —"— 21st	Trench lost by Cavalry + French on our left + Cavalry lost heavily in retaking it – Some amusing incidents with Germans opposite 35 Trench who were only 25 yards away – they threw Newspapers + letters into our Trench + shouted for Cigarettes but got Hand grenades instead.	
—"— —"— 22nd	Relieved KOSBs in the Fire Trenches. Fairly quiet.	
—"— —"— 23rd	Heavy Shelling all day. 2/Lt Slingsby wounded.	
—"— —"— 24th	Heavy shell fire – our HQ shelled – not much damage. Relieved at night by KOSBs + retired to Support Trenches at BLAAUWEPOORT FARM. Draft of one officer (Capt Palmer) + 43 R+F joined Battn.	

(9 26 6) W 257—976 100,000 4/12 H W V 79/3298

Army Form C. 2118.

Instructions regarding War Diaries and Intelligence Summaries are contained in F. S. Regs., Part II. and the Staff Manual respectively. Title pages will be prepared in manuscript.

WAR DIARY
or
INTELLIGENCE SUMMARY.
(*Erase heading not required.*)

Hour, Date, Place		Summary of Events and Information	Remarks and references to Appendices
Support Trenches at BLAAUWPOORT.	Feby 25th	Heavy Fall of Snow. West Kents + Duke of Wellingtons lost 6 officers + 100 men in trench on our left by shell + Minenwerfer Fire.	
Trenches to VLAMERTINGHE	" 26th	Fairly quiet day. Relieved at BLAAUWE POORT by 1st Batt KOYLI under command of Lt Col Ingham Brooke + retired to Huts near VLAMERTINGHE. Casualties during tour in Trenches 1 officer wounded. 6 men killed + 11 wounded.	
VLAMERTINGHE	" 27th	Resting in Huts at VLAMERTINGHE.	
"	" 28th	"	

(9 26 6) W 257—976 100,000 4/12 H W V 79/3298

13th Bde.
5th Div.

2nd K. O. Y. L. I.

....

1 9 1 5

13th Bde.
5th Div.
ATTACHED TO 28th DIV

2nd K. O. Y. L. I.

MARCH

1 9 1 5

[illegible]

Instructions regarding War Diaries and Intelligence Summaries are contained in F. S. Regs., Part II. and the Staff Manual respectively. Title pages will be prepared in manuscript.

WAR DIARY
or
~~INTELLIGENCE SUMMARY.~~

(*Erase heading not required.*)

Army Form C. 2118.

Hour, Date, Place		Summary of Events and Information	Remarks and references to Appendices
To Trenches. at VERBRANDENMOLEN.	March 1st	Marched at 4 P.m. to trenches at VERBRANDENMOLEN via YPRES and relieved 1st Bn KOYLI in Sector C.	
Trenches at VERBRANDENMOLEN	" 2nd	Trenches rather heavily shelled & Bn HQ shelled twice. Not much damage done.	
To YPRES.	" 3rd	Battn withdrew into Support in YPRES leaving A & C Coys as Support to KOSBs who relieved us in the Firing Line.	
at YPRES.	" 4th	Remained in Support in YPRES. Town shelled with High Explosive and Shrapnel during the day.	
To Trenches.	" 5th	Relieved KOSBs in Firing Line at VERBRANDENMOLEN. An unusual amount of Rifle Fire all night but no attack.	
Trenches at VERBRANDENMOLEN	" 6th	Snipers very active on both sides. Also a lot of Hand Grenade throwing & Bombing from 35 Trench which is within 20 yards of German Trenches. Capt H.T. Watson shot through the head by a Sniper & died of wounds.	
YPRES.	" 7th	Battn withdrew to Support in YPRES leaving B & D Coys as Support to KOSB. who relieved us in firing line.	
YPRES	" 8th	Remained in Support in YPRES. Town shelled as usual.	
Trenches at VERBRANDENMOLEN	" 9th	Relieved the KOSBs in the firing line in Sector C.	
Trenches to Reserve near VERBR[ANDENMOLEN]	" 10th	Fairly quiet day & few Casualties. Relieved at night by 5th Fusiliers (9th Infy Bde) & withdrew into Bde Reserve. Casualties from 1st to 10th March 1 officer & 5 men killed & 24 men wounded.	

(9 29 6) W 257—676 100,000 4/12 H W V 3298

Army Form C. 2118.

Instructions regarding War Diaries and Intelligence Summaries are contained in F. S. Regs., Part II. and the Staff Manual respectively. Title pages will be prepared in manuscript.

WAR DIARY
or
INTELLIGENCE SUMMARY.
(*Erase heading not required.*)

Place	Hour, Date, Place	Summary of Events and Information	Remarks and references to Appendices
Reserve at Vlamertinghe.	March 11th	In Divisional Reserve at VLAMERTINGHE –	
– " –	– " – 12th	Draft of 4 Officers (Capt J.J. Wyley – Capt Yates – 2Lt Hunter – 2Lt Hodges) and 19 Men joined the Batt.	
– " –	– " – 13th	2Lt Roberts joined the Batt. – Lines inspected by Corps Commander (Genl Plumer) accompanied by Divl Commander (Genl Bulfin) + Brigadier at 10 am. At 3 P.M. Army Commander (Sir H Smith Dorrien) visited the Batt. + addressed the Officers asking Company Commanders to explain to all their men the reason why the Batt. had been transferred to YPRES. He said that before the arrival of the 13th Infy Bde the enemy had become very aggressive + had to a certain extent become masters of the situation. He consequently thought it necessary to send up troops he could thoroughly rely on + had long experience in the Country + had specially selected the 13th 15th + 9th Brigades for this work. He was glad to say that everything was now just right + the Enemy subdued + the line strengthened. He wished to thank the Batt. for all they had done. The Corps + Divisional Commander thoroughly endorsed all the Army Commander had said + also expressed their thanks to the Batt.	
Vlamertinghe to St ELOI –	– " – 14th	Enemy commenced a heavy bombardment of St ELOI at Dusk followed by Infantry attack with the result that the 27th Divn lost 7 Trenches and the Mound just East of the village. The 13th Infy Bde marched at 9 P.M. to their assistance, the Batt. halting for the night on the road near KRUISTRAAT – We were here informed that the Germans had entered St ELOI + that the 27th Divn were going to counter attack at 2 A.M.	

(9 26 6) W257–976 100,000 4/12 H W V

79
3298

WAR DIARY
or
INTELLIGENCE SUMMARY.
(Erase heading not required.)

Army Form C. 2118.

Instructions regarding War Diaries and Intelligence Summaries are contained in F. S. Regs., Part II. and the Staff Manual respectively. Title pages will be prepared in manuscript.

Hour, Date, Place		Summary of Events and Information	Remarks and references to Appendices
St ELOI.	March 15th	The Counter attack by 27th Divn at 2 am. was only partially Successful so they again attacked at 5 am. driving the Enemy out of St ELOI & retaking the lost trenches with the exception of the Mound and the trenches immediately North & South of it. At Dawn the R W Kent Regt & ~~Duke of Wellington~~ K.O.S.B. retired to YPRES. The KOYLI & ~~K.O.S.B.~~ Duke of Wellington being placed at the disposal of Genl Snow Commanding 27th Divn, The Battn bivouacking in the fields near KRUISTRAAT HOEK. At 1 P.M. the C.O. received orders to report to Br: Genl Longley at VOORMEZEELE to discuss an attack we were to make to retake the Mound that night. After all arrangements had been made this attack was abandoned by order of Genl Snow. At Dusk the Battn moved forward to the woods of a Chateau near VOORMEZEELE after having been shelled most of the day but only losing about 6 men. During the evening orders were received that the Battn would attack a parallel held by the enemy just North of the Mound E of St ELOI at Dusk the following evening. The C.O. consequently sent out 8 officers to reconnoitre the position during the night. During this reconnaissance 2/Lt P. Rohan was killed & the remainder of the party returned at about 4 am.	
St ELOI.	March 16th	At 7 am. The Battn retired to a position about 3/4 mile in rear where we were to remain until we moved to attack at Dusk. At 10.30 am. sudden orders came that the Battn was to retire to VLAMERTINGHE at once & that the attack at Dusk was Cancelled. The Battn reached VLAMERTINGHE at 1 P.M. At 4 P.M. orders were received that the Battn would march at 6 P.M. to relieve the 15th Bde in Sector A. We accordingly marched via YPRES to ROSENTHAL and Lankhof Chateaus where we relieved the Dorset Regt in Support to Sector A. 2/Lt Gamble joined the Battn at Vlamertinghe and Capt Palmer went down sick	

Instructions regarding War Diaries and Intelligence Summaries are contained in F. S. Regs., Part II. and the Staff Manual respectively. Title pages will be prepared in manuscript.

WAR DIARY
or
INTELLIGENCE SUMMARY.
(Erase heading not required.)

Army Form C. 2118.

Hour, Date, Place		Summary of Events and Information	Remarks and references to Appendices
Support Tren[redacted] at Rosenthal Chateau.	St Patricks Day.	Remained in Support to Sector A. Not much Shelling.	
Trenches in Sector A.	March 18th	Relieved K.O.S.B.s in Fire Trenches in Sector A. Bad Sector and very wet Trenches. Heavy firing during night from direction of St Eloi.	
—"—	March 19th	Trenches in Sector A.	
To KRUISTRAAT	March 20th	Relieved at 10 P.m. by K.O.S.B.s & retired to KRUISTRAAT. Shelled all day with "Whiz Bangs". several Killed & wounded. Reached KRUISTRAAT about 12 M.N.	
at KRUISTRAAT	March 21st	In reserve at KRUISTRAAT where we were shelled all day with High Explosives.	
To Trenches in Sector A.	March 22nd	marched at 7P.m. & relieved K.O.S.B.s in Fire Trenches.	
Trenches in Sector A.	March 23rd	In Trenches in Sector A.	
Support at Rosenthal	March 24th	Relieved at [redacted] 10 P.m. by K.O.S.B.s & retired to Support at Rosenthal Chateau.	
at Rosenthal	March 25th	In Support at Rosenthal and Lankhof. Shelled in Morning. Lieut Wells joined Battn	

(9 26 6) W257—976 100,000 4/12 H W V 79/3298

Instructions regarding War Diaries and Intelligence Summaries are contained in F. S. Regs., Part II. and the Staff Manual respectively. Title pages will be prepared in manuscript.

WAR DIARY
or
INTELLIGENCE SUMMARY.
(Erase heading not required.)

Army Form C. 2118.

Hour, Date, Place		Summary of Events and Information	Remarks and references to Appendices
Rosenthal to Vlamertinghe.	March 26th	Relieved at 10 P.m. by Royal Scots Fusiliers and retired to Huts at Vlamertinghe. Lieuts Webb & Way. N Staffords joined Battn.	
at Vlamertinghe	March 27th	In Huts at Vlamertinghe	
"	28th	" 2Lt Dixon joined Battn.	
"	29th	"	
"	30th	"	
Trenches.	31st	Battn moved into the Trenches at Verbranden Molen. (Section C)	

(9 26 6) W257—976 100,000 4/12 H W V 79/3298

13th Bde.
5th Div.

2nd K. O. Y. L. I.

....

1 9 1 5.

13th Brigade.

28th Division (Brigade returned to 5th Division 7. 4. 15.)

2nd BATTALION

KING'S OWN YORKSHIRE LIGHT INFANTRY

APRIL 1915.

2nd KOYLI

Instructions regarding War Diaries and Intelligence Summaries are contained in F. S. Regs., Part II. and the Staff Manual respectively. Title pages will be prepared in manuscript.

WAR DIARY
or
INTELLIGENCE SUMMARY.
(Erase heading not required.)

Army Form C. 2118.

Hour, Date, Place		Summary of Events and Information	Remarks and references to Appendices
Trenches at Verbrandenmolen	April 1st	In Trenches at Verbrandenmolen. Enemy's artillery active but not much damage done.	
—"—	April 2nd	Bn HQ and B Coy retired to YPRES leaving A C + D Coys in woods in support to KOSBs who relieved us in the firing line.	[initials]
—"—	April 3rd	Remained in support to KOSBs. Bishop of London visited YPRES.	
—"—	Easter Day - 4th	Relieved KOSBs in firing line. They remained in support to us. Relief carried out by day for first time.	
—"—	April 5th	In firing line. Enemy brought up large "Minenwerfer" in front of 35 Trench held by D Coy. The Trench was heavily bombed + shelled at intervals throughout the day causing 14 casualties + severely damaging the Trench. Several men were buried also 3 officers (Lt Lee, Gray, Hunter). The latter were unhurt. Our artillery gave us no support.	[initials]
—"—	April 6th	Trench 35 again heavily bombed + shelled. Artillery support more effective but unfortunately one Belgian shell fell short into 36 Trench wounding 5 men of A Coy. Except for this the Belgian artillery fire was very good. Relieved in evening by KOSB + retired into support dugouts. D Coy + Bn HQ retiring to YPRES.	[initials]
—"—	April 7th	In support to KOSBs. At 8 am. a shell hit our Bn HQ in YPRES passing through the room occupied by the Snipers + [illegible] in the kitchen. Pte King + [illegible] killed. Sgt Spooner + 2 others wounded. No officers hurt although there were 6 in the House at the time. Bn HQ moved [illegible] to another part of YPRES. At [illegible]	

(9 26 6) W257—976 100,000 4/12 H.W.V. 79/3298

Instructions regarding War Diaries and Intelligence Summaries are contained in F. S. Regs., Part II. and the Staff Manual respectively. Title pages will be prepared in manuscript.

WAR DIARY

or

INTELLIGENCE SUMMARY.

(Erase heading not required.)

Army Form C. 2118.

Hour, Date, Place		Summary of Events and Information	Remarks and references to Appendices
Trenches	April 7th	Orders came that the Battn would relieve Dorset Regt in Trenches 31 & 32(a) & (b) that night. Moved at 7 p.m. Relief completed at 11.30 p.m.	[initials]
– " –	– " – 8th	In Trenches between VERBRANDEN Molen & Canal. Quiet day. Heavy firing on our left towards the Sea.	
	– " – 9th	In Trenches. Heavy firing again on our left. Lt & Q.M. A.E. Bendam Sent down sick.	
– " –	– " – 10th	Relieved from Trenches by Dorset Regt at 12 M.N. & returned to RENINGHELST to Billets. Long march for the men who did not get in until 6 am 10th. 1st Battn Billeted in YPRES so the 2 Battns again met. The 2nd Battn H.Q. being entertained to Supper by H.Q. 1st Battn on their way from the Trenches.	[initials]
RENINGHELST.	– " – 11th	In Billets Resting.	
		The 5th Division H.Q. and 14th Bde having arrived from BAILLEUL the 13th Bde was Transferred back to its proper Division on 7th April. On the Departure of the 13th Bde from the 28th Division the following letters were received from the 5th Corps & 28 Divl Commanders. (attached)	[initials]
Reninghelst	April 12th, 13th, 14th	In Huts. Resting. [On night of 12th/13th at about 11.30 p.m. a Zeppelin passed over dropping Bombs. No one hurt.] Capt Palmer & 2 Lt R.A.F. joined Battn on 12th	

Instructions regarding War Diaries and Intelligence Summaries are contained in F. S. Regs., Part II. and the Staff Manual respectively. Title pages will be prepared in manuscript.

WAR DIARY
or
INTELLIGENCE SUMMARY.
(Erase heading not required.)

Army Form C. 2118.

Hour, Date, Place		Summary of Events and Information	Remarks and references to Appendices
Reninghelst	April 15th	Resting –	
—"—	—"— 16th	—"— – B= Field day in Morning –	
YPRES –	—"— 17th	Moved to YPRES in connection with operation on HILL 60. At 7 P.M. in 3 series at 10 seconds interval were exploded under HILL 60. The explosion was accompanied by a heavy bombardment of the Hill lasting about 15 minutes immediately after which the Hill was stormed & captured by the R. West Kent Regt, who although they were twice counter attacked & heavily bombed & bombarded held on until relieved by the KOSB's.	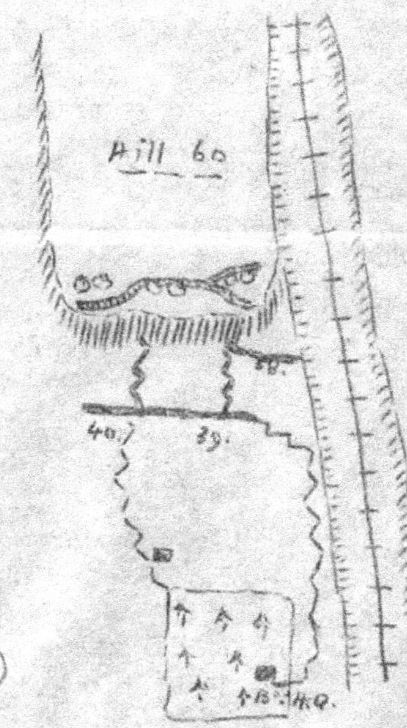
HILL 60	—"— 18th	At Dawn on 18th however a very strong counter attack on the left of the Hill compelled the KOSB. to give way & the Summit was retaken by the Germans. At 7 am. the Battn moved forward from YPRES & replaced the West Riding Regt (who had moved forward to the Hill) under the Railway Embankment in Rear of the Hill where we remained until 12 Noon. In the meantime the West Ridings relieved the KOSB. under the Hill. At 12.30 P.M. the Battn moved forward into a Larch wood just in rear of Hill 60 under heavy shell fire in support to the West Ridings & the West Kents & KOSB's retired behind the Railway. At 3 P.M. orders were received that the Hill must be retaken at all costs, & it fell to the West Ridings & KOYLI to make the assault. The situation & orders for attack were as follows: the West Ridings were in position in dead ground at the bottom of the Hill & also held 39 & 40. Trenches (vide sketch) with the KOYLI in the wood just in rear. At 5 P.M. the West Ridings filtered their men up some communicating Trenches leading to the base of the Hill where they massed. The KOYLI at the same time moved forward from the Larch wood up the Railway cutting & communicating Trench into 39 & 40 Trenches about 80 yards in rear of the bottom of Hill 60. At 6 P.M., at which hour the assault was timed to take place, the West Ridings advanced up the slopes of the Hill & at the same moment B Coy under Capt Alt & C Coy under Capt Kent jumped forward from 39 & 40 Trenches dashed across the open space to the foot of the Hill & up the slopes intermingling with the West Ridings in the assault. A Coy under Capt Yates followed close behind carrying Spades & Hand Grenades. D Coy under Capt Palmer which was waiting behind in the communicating trench to 40 Trench moved up to Garrison Trenches 39 & 40. The whole advance was covered by our artillery who heavily bombarded the Hill & in rear of it to prevent the Germans reinforcing the Hill crest –	[signature]

Instructions regarding War Diaries and Intelligence Summaries are contained in F. S. Regs., Part II. and the Staff Manual respectively. Title pages will be prepared in manuscript.

WAR DIARY
or
INTELLIGENCE SUMMARY.
(Erase heading not required.)

Army Form C. 2118.

Hour, Date, Place	Summary of Events and Information	Remarks and references to Appendices
	B & C Coys immediately they left the Trenches were met with a hail of Artillery, Machine Gun & Rifle fire causing very heavy Casualties. These Coys however reached the base of the Hill & dashing up the slopes carried the West Ridings, who were by that time being hard pressed, forward & after a moments wavering which looked as if the attack would fail, the line crossed the German Parapet & the Crest of the Hill was retaken. The Germans once we got to close quarters fled in a panic down their Communicating Trenches leaving equipment Rifles & ammunition behind them. They could not however get away as their trenches became blocked with their own killed & wounded & most of them were either captured or killed by our rifle fire Bayonets & Hand Grenades. After the capture of the Hill A Coy who had come up with spades & transferred the parapet of the Trench. The Hill though taken had now to be held & throughout the night we were subjected to the concentrated fire of 44 German Battys of Field & heavy Artillery - (a German Observing Officer we captured on the Hill afterwards gave us this information). The Germans also counter attacked continuously using hand Grenades & Bombs & furious combats took place in the Craters made by the explosions of the mines which soon became a shambles & filled with killed & wounded. The Crater on the left we were unable to hold so we entrenched ourselves a few yards behind it, our trench passing in front of the remaining Craters. The German High Explosive Shells gave off blinding & suffocating fumes which caused great distress amongst the men but they hung on. Rifles got jammed from the heat of firing & Grenades & Ammunition were difficult to get up owing to the block of wounded in the communicating & fire trenches & if it had not been for the stacks of German Rifles & ammn left behind which our men used instead of their own it would have been difficult to maintain our position on the Hill which however we did until relieved at Dawn on 19th April by the Bedford Regt. After relief the Battn retired into the woods in rear of 35 Trench.	
	During the 19th April the Enemy again gained a footing on the left crest of the Hill but a counter attack by the 9th Q.V. Rifles (the last remaining Batt of	

Instructions regarding War Diaries and Intelligence Summaries are contained in F. S. Regs., Part II. and the Staff Manual respectively. Title pages will be prepared in manuscript.

WAR DIARY
or
INTELLIGENCE SUMMARY.
(*Erase heading not required.*)

Army Form C. 2118.

Hour, Date, Place			Summary of Events and Information	Remarks and references to Appendices
			of the 13th Infty Brigade) dislodged them again & the Hill was finally secured. The Casualties incurred in the assault were heavy especially amongst officers & the proportion of officers killed to wounded was abnormal.	[initials]
			Casualties. ~~[illegible]~~	
			Officers. Killed. Capts: Alt. Leather.	
			Lieuts. Childs. Williams. Hodges. Oldham. Chubb.	
			Died of Wounds. Capt. Yates. Wyley	[initials]
			Wounded. Capt. Kent.	
			Lts. Wells. Dixon. Upton. Way. Webb.	
			Rank & File. Killed 25. Wounded 190. Missing 10.	
	April	19th	In woods in rear of No 35 Trench. Rested & Bivouacked for the Night. Heavy shelling on Hill 60 & on Dump near Verbrandenmolen.	
To OUDERDOM Huts.	—"—	20th	Marched from woods at 10.30 am. to OUDERDOM Huts. Gen Smith-Dorrien. Genl Ferguson & Genl Morland all called in to Congratulate Colonel Withycombe on Success of our attack on Hill 60. Draft of 52 R&F joined Bn	
At Ouderdom.		21st	Br Genl Wanless O'Gowan paraded Bn to Congratulate us on recapture of Hill 60 & addressed the Batt as follows:– (vide attached marked (A) & attachments) Capt King joined Battn	
Ouderdom towards YPRES.		22nd	At 2.30 Pm. the Commander in Chief assembled the 13th Infty Bde on our parade Ground. He was accompanied by Sir H Smith-Dorrien. Genl Ferguson. Genl Morland & Br Genl Wanless O'Gowan. The C in C address the Brigade in the following terms:– (vide attached marked (B).) At 7 P.M. the Battn marched out with the intention of relieving the Dorset Regt in Sector C. As soon as we reached the YPRES-Poperinghe Road we were met by a continual Stream of Refugees coming from YPRES followed by French Algerian troops & transport of all sorts which completely blocked the road & our further march forward. We then learnt that the Germans had used asphyxiating gasses on the French Algerian troops trenches between the Yser Canal & St Julien & that they had left their entire line of trenches & that the Germans had broken through & were advancing on YPRES. Also that the retirement of the Algerians had left the Canadian Line in the air & that they had been also compelled to retire. These rumours: all proved eventually to be only too true.	[initials]

(9 26 6) W257—976 100,000 4/12 H W V 79/3298

Instructions regarding War Diaries and Intelligence Summaries are contained in F. S. Regs., Part II. and the Staff Manual respectively. Title pages will be prepared in manuscript.

WAR DIARY
or
INTELLIGENCE SUMMARY.
(Erase heading not required.)

Army Form C. 2118.

Hour, Date, Place		Summary of Events and Information	Remarks and references to Appendices
	1915	(Continued from Book I.)	
Ouderdom towards YPRES.	April 22nd	too true & eventually the 13th Infty Bde were ordered not to proceed to relieve the 15th Bde but to Bivouack in the fields south of the YPRES-VLAMERTINGHE ROAD where we spent the rest of the night. Major Gowans, Lts Clarke & Woodbrooke joined the 2nd Bn on transfer from 1st Bn.	
attached to 1st Canadian Divn in Operations N.E. of YPRES.	" 23rd	At 8am orders were received placing the 13th Infty Bde at the disposal of 1st Canadian Divn (Genl Alderson) in 5th Corps. & at 9am the Bde marched via VLAMERTINGHE to some fields near BRIELEN where we halted for some 2 hours. We now learnt that the Germans had advanced during the night as far as the Ponton Bridge over the Canal West of BRIELEN [& in doing so had captured 44 French Guns & 2 4.7" Howitzers (British),] but that the Canadians had driven them back somewhat [& recovered the Howitzers]. As the enemy were still occupying a line ~~[illegible]~~ south of PILKEM from the Canal towards St JULIEN the French had been ordered to attack & drive them back & reoccupy PILKEM. As however it was doubtful whether this attack had developed at all the 13th Infty Bde were ordered to attack at 5 p.m. from the Ponton Bridge W of BRIELAN & push on as far as possible towards PILKEM, the direction of attack being due north with our left on the Canal & our right on the YPRES-PILKEM ROAD. This attack was to cooperate with an attack to be made by 3 Bns under Colonel Geddes (Buffs) who was to have his left on the YPRES-PILKEM ROAD. At 5 p.m. the attack started, the firing line being formed with the K.O.S.B. on Right & R.W.Kents on left. The K.O.Y.L.I. in close support moved in rear of the West Kents with the 9th Q.V. Rifles in reserve. The West Ridings had been sent	

(73989) W4141—463. 400,000. 9/14. H.&J.Ltd. Forms/C. 2118/10.

Instructions regarding War Diaries and Intelligence Summaries are contained in F. S. Regs., Part II. and the Staff Manual respectively. Title pages will be prepared in manuscript.

WAR DIARY
or
INTELLIGENCE SUMMARY.
(*Erase heading not required.*)

Army Form C. 2118.

Hour, Date, Place	Summary of Events and Information	Remarks and references to Appendices
	Sent back to OUDER DOM to re organize after Hill 60 + was not with the Brigade. When the attack developed the KOSB although suffering heavily pushed the enemy back on the right. The advance of the RW Kents on the left however was delayed by lines of French troops advancing across their front. These turned out to be the Regts which had been supposed to have attacked earlier in the day but had not done so + only started to advance when they saw the 13th Infy Bde advancing in the morning. By 7 p.m. however the West Kents by inclining to their right had pushed on in line with the French on their left + had reinforced the KOSB who had been greatly thinned out. By night-fall a line was established with the Canal on the left + St JULIEN on the right but PILKEM was still in the hands of the enemy. After dark the KOYLI moved up with shovels & the line was consolidated.	
April 24th	At Dawn we were relieved in this new trench line by 4th Rifle Bde + withdrew to the Canal Bank near the Pontoon Bridge. At 12 noon the Battn got sudden orders to proceed at once to assist the 10th Canadian Bde in retaking the lost line N.E. of WIELTJE. We marched at once followed by the Q.V. Rifles + on approaching St JEAN were subjected to a very heavy shell fire which followed us until we eventually reached our allotted position in part of the G.H.Q. line of Trenches 500x N.E. of WIELTJE where we had to crowd into a trench already filled with Canadian Highlanders. Owing to bad Staff arrangements by the Canadian Divn the line which should have been empty + ready for occupation was so crowded with troops of different Regts that our Companies had to lie out in the open fully exposed to the enemy who opened a heavy shrapnel fire + was killing Lt Hunter	[signature]

(73989) W4141—463. 400,000. 9/14. H.&J.Ltd. Forms/C. 2118/10.

Instructions regarding War Diaries and Intelligence Summaries are contained in F. S. Regs., Part II. and the Staff Manual respectively. Title pages will be prepared in manuscript.

WAR DIARY
or
INTELLIGENCE SUMMARY.
(Erase heading not required.)

Army Form C. 2118.

Place	Hour, Date	Summary of Events and Information	Remarks and references to Appendices
		& many men & wounding Lieut Webb & many more. The Q.V.R also suffered very heavily owing to having to lie out in the open. Capt Palmer was also wounded before reaching St JEAN.	W.D.H.
With Canadian Divn.	April 25th	At 3.30 a.m. an attack to retake St JULIEN commenced headed by the 10th Bde. The KOYLI now only 250 strong remained in reserve. By 9 a.m. we had occupied FORTUIN & later the 10th Bde entered St JULIEN but were unable to hold it & at nightfall the Germans still held St JULIEN & the large wood due West of it. A Draft of 108 R&F arrived at A Line for Battn.	W.D.H.
—"—	—"— 26th	At 1 a.m. received orders to retire to reserve at St JEAN where we dug ourselves in & were subjected to heavy shell fire all day. At 2 p.m. the Lahore Divn which had been brought up from the South covered by a very heavy bombardment attacked St JULIEN & the wood to the West of the village. The following officers joined the Battn: Major C.E. Heathcote. 2/Lts Dunn. Thom. Gosschalk. White. Chubb. Glover.	W.D.H.
—"—	—"— 27th	In Reserve at St JEAN where we were heavily shelled all day with High Explosive & Shrapnel. Considering the violence of the bombardment the Battn suffered wonderfully little although we had to move A & C Coys further to the rear.	W.D.H.
—"—	28th	In reserve at St JEAN. Shelled the same as yesterday. Major Gowans wounded by shrapnel. French & Lahore Divs attacked without any apparent result & suffered heavily. Drafts of 65 & 13 R&F arrived at A Line for Bn.	

(73989) W4141—463. 400,000. 9/14. H.&J.Ltd. Forms/C. 2118/10.

Instructions regarding War Diaries and Intelligence Summaries are contained in F. S. Regs., Part II. and the Staff Manual respectively. Title pages will be prepared in manuscript.

WAR DIARY
or
INTELLIGENCE SUMMARY.
(Erase heading not required.)

Army Form C. 2118.

Hour, Date, Place			Summary of Events and Information	Remarks and references to Appendices
attached to 1st Canadian Divn	April	29th	In reserve at St JEAN. Heavy artillery duel all day. Battn moved up at dusk & relieved the K.O.S.B. in the firing line.	[signature]
—"—	—"—	30th	In fire trenches N of WIELTJE. French made progress on our left & along Canal. Quiet day as far as we were concerned. Relieved at night by Essex Regt (4th Div 13th B[de]) & retired to a farm N.W. of BRIELAN which we reached at 3 am. having been shelled the whole way but only losing 5 men.	[signature]
—"—	May	1st	Marched again at 4.30 a.m. to woods N.W. of VLAMERTINGHE where we bivouacked in the woods in perfect weather.	[signature]
—"—	—"—	2nd	Battn spent a pleasant morning resting in the woods but at 5 p.m. we got sudden orders to move out & take up a position S.W. of BRIELAN along a stream as the enemy were attacking N.E. of YPRES. Got in to position at 8 p.m. & remained there until 1 a.m. when we returned to bivouacks in woods which we reached at 3 a.m.	
—"—	—"—	3rd	Rested in the woods until 4 p.m. when we again got orders to move out to the same position S.W. of BRIELAN as last night where we spent the night in pours of rain. 2/Lt Rose joined the Battn	

(A)

Address to Bn by Br Genl Wanless O'Gowan 21/4/15.

CO & Fellow comrades, Officers, NCOs & men of 2nd K.O.Y.L.I. I have come here this morning to congratulate you on the magnificent way in which you attacked & took Hill 60. It is to my mind the finest piece of work the 13th Infty Bde has done which is saying a great deal!

I have received many congratulations – one from the C in C Sir John French – Genl Sir H Smith Dorrien & Genl Sir Charles Fergusson.

I am proud to have the 2/K.O.Y.L.I. in my Brigade. We all deplore the loss of our brave comrades who have so willingly sacrificed their lives.

The latest news is that the enemy has made several heavy attacks to take the Hill back again last night & they have managed to dislodge those occupying the left piece of the Crater – and the honour of taking this back again is again with the 13th Infty Bde – The old Queen Victoria Rifles have been sent to kick them out & I know they will do it.

We are going out again tomorrow night to the trenches & we take on the job given to us & will see it through –

It is a responsible task, & I feel sure that you all will in the future respond to any emergency as you have always done in the past.

(B)

Address to 13th Infty Bde (& other Regts attached)

on 22.4.15.

Officers. N.C.O.s & men of the 13th Infty Bde. K.O.S.B. R.W.K.

2 K.O.Y.L.I. E Surrey Regt. R.E. & Mining Company.

It is in some respects a sad sight that I see before me

a yet at the same time a glorious one. Sad because you

are so few in number compared to what you were a

week ago but after all because I speak of victory

it is a glorious sight.

This is the first opportunity I have had of seeing you

& saying how deeply & truly I appreciate your magnificent

work & the operation of bringing to a glorious conclusion

a great & important plan with far reaching results.

The operation was planned by Lt Genl Bulfin who

knew the ground so well & it was ably planned &

carried out. It fell to you to carry it through & on

17th April at 7 P.M. 6 mines were exploded under the

enemy's trenches on Hill 60. The Hill had to be taken

& the West Kents & K.O.S.B. were chosen to take it.

These two Regts gallantly & splendidly advanced & took

the position. But they knew that the taking of it was

only the smallest part of the work to be done. All through

that long night they were subjected to the terrific

fire of the enemy's artillery. That piece of ground

was very important to either side. It is good as an

artillery observation post. It is useful to us but it

was of much more importance to the enemy. From it

he can observe all the surrounding country back to

YPRES & thus we knew that on account of its great

importance he would put up a stubborn fight to regain it

and whatever we may say against the Germans they are brave courageous men & worthy of our steel. And early next morning found the West Kents & K.O.S.B. repelling attack after attack with the utmost gallantry & tenacity. At last it was necessary to ~~take~~ relieve them though they would have stayed to the last man so the K.O.Y.L.I. & West Ridings were sent up, & it was the same that ~~[illegible]~~ them. Violent attack after attack was delivered against them with the same gallantry & tenacity as the other two battalions they held the position for 36 hours & threw the enemy back time after time with heavy loss. Then came the time to relieve them & the Bedfords & East Surrey Regt took their place, & again the same attacks & again the same loss to the enemy. Yet this does not tell one hundredth or one thousandth part of all that you did.

I can only thank you with all my heart men. I thank Genl Smith-Dorrien, I thank Genl Sir Charles Fergusson, Genl Morland & Br Genl O'Gowan.

Here again let me say though your casualty lists have been heavy your officers are in greater proportion than the N.C.O.s & men. They go forward like true British soldiers knowing that you will follow them. That is the secret of the greatness of our success & it will live for ever.

I have heard it said that Education & Temperance has lowered the standard of our Army & that unless you carry on as we did you will not be as good a campaigns to the size of the Crimea or Peninsular.

You have proved & given a lie to that statement & that is what this campaign has brought out, & the higher the moral tone of the men the greater will be our success. So I leave you something to think about.

Well Officers when I return to you my warmest thanks & express my deep admiration at your magnificent courage & I am sure that you will do all that is required of you.

13th Bde.
5th Div.

2nd K. O. Y. L. I.

MAY.

1 9 1 5.

Army Form C. 2118.

Instructions regarding War Diaries and Intelligence Summaries are contained in F. S. Regs., Part II. and the Staff Manual respectively. Title pages will be prepared in manuscript.

WAR DIARY
or
INTELLIGENCE SUMMARY.

(Erase heading not required.)

Place	Date	Hour	Summary of Events and Information	Remarks and references to Appendices
Attached to 1 Canadian Div				
	April 29"			

(A9475) Wt W2358/P360 600,000 12/17 D. D. & L. Sch. 52a. Forms/C2118/15.

Army Form C. 2118.

WAR DIARY
or
INTELLIGENCE SUMMARY.
(Erase heading not required.)

Instructions regarding War Diaries and Intelligence Summaries are contained in F. S. Regs., Part II, and the Staff Manual respectively. Title pages will be prepared in manuscript.

Place	Date	Hour	Summary of Events and Information	Remarks and references to Appendices
Attached to 1st Canadian Di				
	1st May		Marched again at 4.30 am to Woods N.W. of VLAMERTINGHE where we bivouacked in the woods in perfect weather.	
	2nd	"	Battalion spent a pleasant morning resting in the woods but at 5 am we got sudden orders to move out & take up a position S.W. of BRIELAN along a stream as the enemy were attacking NE of YPRES. Got into position at 8 pm & remained there until 1 am when we returned to bivouack in woods which we reached at 3 am.	
	3rd	"	Rested in the woods until 4 pm when we again got orders to move out to the same position S.W. of BRIELAN as last night where we spent the night in Pours of Rain. 2/Lt ROE joined the Battn.	

(A9475) Wt W2358/P360 600,000 12/17 D. D. & L. Sch. 52a. Forms/C2118/15.

Instructions regarding War Diaries and Intelligence Summaries are contained in F. S. Regs., Part II. and the Staff Manual respectively. Title pages will be prepared in manuscript.

Army Form C. 2118.

WAR DIARY
or
INTELLIGENCE SUMMARY.
(Erase heading not required.)

Hour, Date, Place		Summary of Events and Information	Remarks and references to Appendices
Attached to Canadian Div.	May 4th	Received orders at Dawn to retire to Huts near OUDERDOM (Sapper Town) where the Batt. arrived at 6 a.m. & were promised 3 or 4 days rest. – The attached letter & wire from G.O.C. 5th Corps & G.O.C. 1st Canadian Div. (marked (A) (B) respectively) were received on our leaving the Canadians to rejoin 5th Div. –	[signature]
Rejoined 5th Div.	–"– 5th	at 9 a.m. heard news that HILL 60 & the ZWARTELEEN SALIENT had been lost, the Enemy again using Asphyxiating Gasses with appalling results. Called out at 1 P.m. & marched to CHATEAU near KRUISTRAAT where we halted until 4 P.m. & then marched to trenches in G.H.Q. line between Canal & Railway Embankment S.E. of YPRES. at dusk the Bn moved again under cover of Railway Embankment close to 13th & 15th Bde H.Q. to act in support to West Kent Regt & K.O.S.B. who were attacking the ZWARTELEEN SALIENT and HILL 60 respectively. These attacks however failed as although the K.O.S.B. got to the top of the HILL the attack of the West Kents on the Salient was unable to progress & HILL 60 was consequently untenable. The consequence was that the K.O.S.B. after having practically retaken HILL 60, though with heavy loss, had to evacuate it again leaving the line the same as it had been before. The K.O.Y.L.I. did not move forward but remained for the night in their position under the Railway Embankment where we obtained good cover from the many shells that came our way.	[signature]
	–"– 6th		

(73989) W4141—463. 400,000. 9/14. H.&J.Ltd. Forms/C. 2118/10.

WAR DIARY
or
INTELLIGENCE SUMMARY.

(Erase heading not required.)

Army Form C. 2118.

Instructions regarding War Diaries and Intelligence Summaries are contained in F. S. Regs., Part II. and the Staff Manual respectively. Title pages will be prepared in manuscript.

(a)

Hour, Date, Place	Summary of Events and Information	Remarks and references to Appendices
Attack on ZWARTELEEN SALIENT. May 6th	A Hot Sunny day. At about Noon the Colonel received a notification that the Battn was to make an attack during the night or at Dawn on the ZWARTELEEN SALIENT & the Brigadier asked him to reconnoitre the position & let him know how he considered the attack could best be made. Consequently at 2 P.M. the C.O. 2nd i/c (?) Adjt & 4 Coy Commdrs set out to get a view of the Salient from 41 Trench. As a result of this reconnaissance the attached orders for attack were issued by Brigadier at 6.5 P.M. (marked (A)). After receipt of these orders the C.O. assembled all officers & explained his dispositions for the attack which were as follows:- (reference rough sketch below) The Enemy held HILL 60 & the ZWARTELEEN SALIENT and all the line of trench marked XXXXX. They had also dug a new trench across the neck of the Salient	[signature]
—"— May 7th	(a) & occupied it. At (B) a Barrier had been erected by both sides. The Cheshire Regt held 38. 39. & 40 Trenches & the Royal Irish Rifles 46 Trench. The Cheshires also occupied 41 Trench. At 2.30 a.m. at which time the K.O.Y.L.I. were to attack the Batt. Battn was to be in position as follows:- The 2 assaulting Coys B & A under Command of Capt King & 2/Lt Roberts respectively were to be massed in 41 Trench. C Coy with shovels & sandbags were to be in Communicating Trench (C) (under Lt Singleton), ready to move up & fill in B & A Coys in the attack. D Coy to be in rear of C (under Lt Clarke) also to move up into 41 Trench to either reinforce the attack or remain in 41 as required. At 2.30 a.m. the Barrier (B) which had been mined was to be blown up & the Cheshires in 40 assisted by Bombing Parties of K.O.S.B. & West Kents were to push up into 43 & assist our attack, the R.I.R. doing the same from 46 on the left. The Head of each of these parties were to show us their position by a flash light. The Batt paraded under the Railway Embankment at 11.45 P.M. & moved up along the railway & by 2 a.m. was all ready in the above positions. At the appointed hour (2.30 a.m.) although the explosion of the Barrier did not take place B Coy closely followed by A Coy jumped forward over the parapet of 41 & advanced direct on new German Trench (a). After they had gone about 10x they were met with a terrific Rifle & Machine Gun fire & were mowed down fast. They however reached & took Trench (a) & crossed into the Salient. They were followed by C Coy & later by D Coy. The latter however in the dark was lost direction & inclining too much to their right got into 40 Trench. Meanwhile the Barrier at (B) exploded	

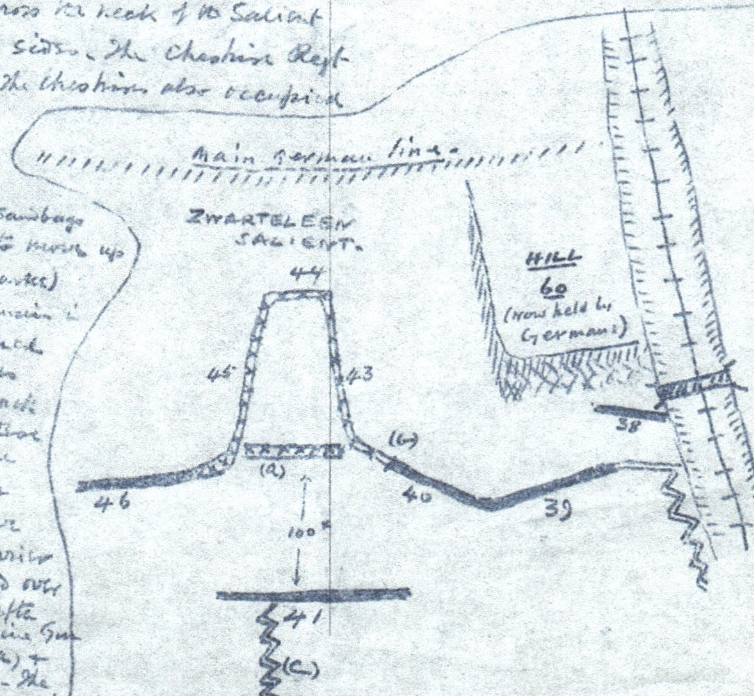

Instructions regarding War Diaries and Intelligence Summaries are contained in F. S. Regs., Part II. and the Staff Manual respectively. Title pages will be prepared in manuscript.

WAR DIARY
or
INTELLIGENCE SUMMARY.
(Erase heading not required.)

Army Form C. 2118.

Hour, Date, Place	Summary of Events and Information	Remarks and references to Appendices

although some what late & the Cheshires pushed forward some 70^x up into the Salient. Nothing was seen or heard of the R.I.R. on the left & they gave no assistance. The first reliable information to come back was from Lt Roberts who came in wounded & stated that the 1st Trench (a) had been taken & crossed & that B & A Coys were well up in the SALIENT. Shortly after this Dawn broke & it became evident that although the Enemy had been driven out of the neck of the Salient they still held the Salient itself. It also became evident that any of A, B, or C Coys who had got through would not be able to communicate back or move until nightfall.
The Cheshire Regt who had advanced well up in the Salient on the right had been bombed back again to their old position & had re-established the blown up Barrier.
The day passed fairly quietly & without any news from the Salient which caused a feeling of suspense all round. Darkness came at 7.45 P.m. & patrols were sent out to look for wounded men & to try and ascertain what the result of the attack had been. The situation, although it was known that the attack had failed, was not cleared up until Capt King crawled in slightly wounded & gave the following narrative:– (attached marked (A)). From Capt Kings narrative it is evident that only small portion of A. B & C Coys lived to enter the Salient & as only a sprinkling of these Coys ever turned up the remainder must have been either killed, wounded, or captured. Unfortunately there can be no doubt that many ^wounded^ men died lying out unable to get back. In fact as late as 12th May 3 men crawled into our Trench. Two of these died of exposure before they could say anything. The third declared that there was a party of one Officer & about 14 men in an old trench in the Salient quite close to the enemy & that they were living on raw potatoes & water. They refused to surrender & when ever the Germans advanced to take them they fired on them. He stated that they had no hope of getting back. As the narrator of this story died shortly after telling it the truth of this could never be verified. If true the officer must have been either Lt Singleton or 2/Lt [illegible]. Casualties in the attack were as follows:–

Instructions regarding War Diaries and Intelligence Summaries are contained in F. S. Regs., Part II. and the Staff Manual respectively. Title pages will be prepared in manuscript.

WAR DIARY
or
INTELLIGENCE SUMMARY.
(Erase heading not required.)

Army Form C. 2118.

Hour, Date, Place		Summary of Events and Information	Remarks and references to Appendices
(Contd)	May 7th	Killed. Lt F. W. Snape + 21 N.C.O.s + Men. Wounded. Lts Roberts - Thorn - Lumb - White - Gosselalk - Clarke - Roe. Capt King - + 116 N.C.O.s + Men. Missing. Lts Singleton - Addenbrooke. + 40 N.C.O.s + Men. Total 11 officers + 177 R+F. The Battn was relieved at night by the S. Lancashire Regt + retired again to the Railway Embankment near Bde H. Qrs.	
Railway Embankmt near ZILLEBEEKE.	May 8th	Shelled all day. Heavy fighting near HOOGE + North of MENIN ROAD.	
—"—	May 9th	Under Railway Embankment near ZILLEBEEKE - More heavy fighting near HOOGE + very heavy Artillery Bombardment. Heard that 1st Battn had been badly cut up. Line maintained - All quiet in our Sector + on Hill 60. Two Hundred men out digging at night.	
—"—	May 10th	Under Railway Embankment - Hot Sunny day + quiet in our Sector. 4th Bde + 27th + 28th Divns. Heavily attacked on our left but they held their line. 200 men out digging at night. A Draft of 418 R+F joined the Battn but No Officers.	
To Huts at SapperTown.	May 11th	Under Cover of Railway Embankment. Relieved at night by K.O.S.B. + returned to Huts at SAPPERTON near Ouderdom. On arrival there however we found that the Norfolk Regt had received no orders to move out + consequently the two Battns were there together. Major R.H. Ellis. Capt Buckle Lieut Palmer (Y+L Regt) 2nd Lt Garnard. Alexander + Butler joined the Battn.	
SapperTown.	—"— 12	Norfolks moved out at 7 a.m. + we moved in to Huts.	

(73989) W4141—463. 400,000. 9/14. H.&J.Ltd. Forms/C. 2118/10.

Instructions regarding War Diaries and Intelligence Summaries are contained in F. S. Regs., Part II. and the Staff Manual respectively. Title pages will be prepared in manuscript.

WAR DIARY
or
INTELLIGENCE SUMMARY.
(Erase heading not required.)

Army Form C. 2118.

Hour, Date, Place		Summary of Events and Information	Remarks and references to Appendices
Sapper Town Huts.	May 13th	2Lt Wells rejoined the Battalion. Resting in Huts at Sapper Town.	
—"—	14th	In Huts at Sapper Town.	[signature]
	15th	—"— a draft of 75 R.F. arrived to join Batt.n under	
—"—	16th	Major Goodwin who left to join his own Regt (2nd Devons). Capt Evans Smith (D.L.I.) & 2Lt Stewart (D.L.I.) joined Batt.n. Major Heathcote left to take command of 1st Batt.n vice Major Brodkey (wounded).	
ZILLEBEKE POND.	17th	Batt.n received sudden orders to move to ZILLEBEKE Pond. Marched out at 6 P.m. & relieved 6th Liverpool Regt at 9 P.m. & came under orders of 8th Brigade. 2nd Lt Gurrey (Queens) joined Batt.n.	
—"—	18th	At ZILLEBEKE POND. 400 men out digging by day & 200 by night on new line from Hill 60 to ZILLEBEKE. Wet day & very uncomfortable for men in the open. Five men wounded whilst digging.	
—"—	19th	Wet day. 400 men out digging by day & 100 by night on new line.	[signature]
To Sapper Town	20th	Fine bright day. Parties out digging all day. Relieved at night by 6th Liverpool Regt & returned to Huts at Sapper Town. 2/Lt Donnelly (Queens) joined Batt.n.	
at Sapper Town.	21st	At Sapper Town Resting.	
—"—	22nd	—"—	
—"—	23rd	—"— Lt Oxstrey & Lt Wein (R. Berks Regt) joined Bn.	
—"—	24th	Batt.n was inspected by Lt Genl Plumer who representing the C in C addressed us as follows:- Col Witts, and the officers & men of K.O.Y.L.I. I am sorry in one way & not in another that your Brigadier is not present here today. He being at home for a well earned rest. During the past month a great deal of	[signature]

Instructions regarding War Diaries and Intelligence Summaries are contained in F. S. Regs., Part II. and the Staff Manual respectively. Title pages will be prepared in manuscript.

WAR DIARY
or
INTELLIGENCE SUMMARY.

(*Erase heading not required.*)

Army Form C. 2118.

Hour, Date, Place	Summary of Events and Information	Remarks and references to Appendices
	Hard, strenuous, & continuous fighting has taken place North of YPRES. this fighting the 13th Infty Bde was suddenly called upon to take part in. It commenced with Hill 60. The attack on which you so successfully carried through. The C in C visited you recently & expressed his great appreciation of the splendid work of the 13th Infty Bde. Immediately after this you were transferred to another area into the great Battle which is known as the 2nd Battle of YPRES. and with the same spirit you enabled us to stay the successful rush of the Enemy. You were then sent back for a well earned rest but it was not yet to be for matters were such in your own area that your services were at once requisitioned for again near Hill 60. It is impossible for the C in C to visit all the Battns & Brigades with all the work he has to do. He did visit the other day the Battns & Brigades of 27th & 28th Divisions & the Canadians & spoke to them & appreciated their splendid work & what he said to them applied equally to you who took part with them throughout. On that occasion the C in C wished all the troops to understand that the great & splendid opposition offered by them in this great Battle which was so successful was far reaching. Its influence went to many States in Europe. Germany had done all in her power to push us back on YPRES & if possible further back well knowing that their success would have meant a good deal to them. But thanks to the spirit & opposition of our troops Italy has declared war on Austria. The C in C explained that at the time this great Battle commenced Genl Joffre & himself had planned a combined attack down South & they had succeeded	[illegible]

(73989) W4141—463. 400,000. 9/14. H.&J.Ltd. Forms/C. 2118/10.

Instructions regarding War Diaries and Intelligence Summaries are contained in F. S. Regs., Part II. and the Staff Manual respectively. Title pages will be prepared in manuscript.

WAR DIARY
or
INTELLIGENCE SUMMARY.
(Erase heading not required.)

Army Form C. 2118.

Hour, Date, Place		Summary of Events and Information	Remarks and references to Appendices
		in making headway & taking a good deal [illegible] from the enemy. Had he been compelled to send troops North to stay the on rush of the Germans at that time, the success of the attack down South would not have been attained. Although the 13th Infty Bde was not part of the original garrison North of YPRES you were called upon to make counter attacks & when the attack could not be pushed any further how nobly & strenuously you held your ground & helped us. These local attacks may seem to have little meaning or result but in this case it enabled us to form our line. The C in C has not time to express his great appreciation of what you have all done, & you will allow me to add mine. When the true facts of Heroism are revealed in History to the world of the 2nd Battle of YPRES I feel sure there will be no honour you will be more proud of on your Regtl Colours.	W.B. Day
Sapper Town	May 25th	Resting in Huts	
To Trenches at St ELOI.	" 26th	Battn moved at 8 P.m. & relieved 1st Fusiliers (9th Bde) in Trenches at St ELOI.	
St ELOI.	" 27th	In Trenches at St ELOI – Everything very quiet & very few Casualties.	W.B. Day
–"–	28th	In Trenches of St ELOI.	
Dickebush Huts	29th	Battn was relieved at night by West Ridings & retired into Support at Huts near DICKEBUSH.	
–"–	30th	In Support near DICKEBUSH.	W.B. Day
–"–	31st	–"–	

(73989) W4141—463. 400,000. 9/14. H.&J.Ltd. Forms/C. 2118/10.

15th Bde.
5th Div.

2nd K. O. Y. L. I.

JUNE

1 9 1 5.

Instructions regarding War Diaries and Intelligence Summaries are contained in F. S. Regs., Part II. and the Staff Manual respectively. Title pages will be prepared in manuscript.

WAR DIARY
or
INTELLIGENCE SUMMARY.
(Erase heading not required.)

2 K.O.Y.L.I.

Army Form C. 2118.

Hour, Date, Place		Summary of Events and Information	Remarks and references to Appendices
Dickebusch to St Eloi Trenches	June 1st	To Trenches at St Eloi defences. Marched at 8 pm & relieved West Kents. Everything very quiet.	[signature]
Trenches at St Eloi	" 2nd	Very quiet.	
"	" 3rd	Col Prior Comdg 9th R West Kents (K2) arrived for instruction. Maj Rigg & Capt Penny (6th K.O.Y.L.I.) also came out to see the Trenches. Maj Rigg stopped the night also Col Prior.	
"	" 4th	Trenches at St Eloi Col Prior, Maj Rigg, CO & Self went round all the Trenches. Maj Rigg left us in afternoon. 2Lt Hicks & 2Lt Dugdale joined Battn.	[signature]
"	" 5th	Trenches at St Eloi. Col Prior left us. Quiet Day. Col Chamberlain Capt Burke & 1 Coy 9th KRR (K1) attached to Bn for instruction.	
"	" 6th	2/Lt De Chesnes joined Bn. Trenches to Dickebusch Huts. Relieved by West Ridings at 11.30 pm.	2/Lt de Longueuil & 2/Lt Milne joined Battn.
Dickebusch Huts. "	" 7th	In support at Dickebusch Huts. 6th K.O.Y.L.I. encamped near us	
"	" 8th	— " —	
" to Trenches at St Eloi.	" 9th	Moved at 8 pm to Trenches at St Eloi & relieved R. West Kents. Major Rigg 6th K.O.Y.L.I. accompanied us for instruction, also 1 Coy 9th K.R.R. (K1).	Capt J.E. Mumby joined Battn.
Trenches at St Eloi.	" 10th	Quiet Day. No Pte Roe 2/K.O.Y.L.I. was shot for Desertion by firing Party of R.W. Kents at 5 am, at Dickebusch Huts.	
"	11th	Trenches at St Eloi. 20 R of F joined Bn	
	12th	— " — 6 — " —	
"	13th	— " —	[signature]
"	14th	— " — Col Gabbett 9th East Lancs (K2) attached to us for 3 days for instruction	
"	15th	Trenches at St Eloi. Things rather more active owing to operations by 5th Corps on our left near HOOGE. Took various measures to lead enemy to suppose that we were contemplating an attack from St Eloi. Germans showed distinct uneasiness in consequence & shelled more than usual.	

(73989) W4141—463. 400,000. 9/14. H.&J.Ltd. Forms/C. 2118/10.

Instructions regarding War Diaries and Intelligence Summaries are contained in F. S. Regs., Part II. and the Staff Manual respectively. Title pages will be prepared in manuscript.

WAR DIARY
or
INTELLIGENCE SUMMARY.
(Erase heading not required.)

Army Form C. 2118.

Hour, Date, Place		Summary of Events and Information	Remarks and references to Appendices
St ELOI to Dickebush Huts.	June 16th	at Dawn 5th Corps attacked on our left taking 3 lines of German Trenches + 200 Prisoners. Heavy Bombardment at Dawn + Dusk. Relieved at 11.30 P.m. by West Ridings ~~Bde~~ and retired to Dickebush Huts.	[initials]
Dickebush Huts	" 17th	at Dickebush Huts. Col Gabbett left. 1st Battn encamped near us at LA CLYTTE. Colonel + adjt went to lunch with them. 2/Lt S. Hallam 2/KOYLI joined Bn.	
"	" 18th	Dickebush Huts.	
St ELOI Defences.	19th	marched at 8 P.m. + relieved Royal West Kents in St ELOI Sector.	
"	20th	Very quiet. only a little shelling by both sides by day + Night.	[initials]
"	21st	Bombardment at 7.30 P.m. by 5th Corps on our left + attack at 8 P.m. Capt H.A.P. Littledale joined Battn.	
"	22nd	Quiet Day. Bar shelling at intervals by day + night. Capt Munby left for 14th Divn Staff.	
	23rd	" " "	
"	24th	Enemy shelled our reserves + Supports. Lieut Palmer + 2/Lt Butler wounded by German Rifle Grenade.	
To Dickebush Huts.	25th	Germans shelled our Supports + reserves. 10 men wounded. 2/Lt Weiss left to join Mining Coy R.E.	
DICKEBUSH Huts.	26th	In Huts resting.	
"	27th	"	
St ELOI DEFENSES	28th	Marched to trenches at 8 P.m. + relieved West Kent Regt.	[initials]
"	29		
"	30	On the whole a quiet time. occasional bursts of shelling on both sides only causing few casualties on our side. Mining + Countermining going on continuously generally in our favour.	
"	July 1st.		
"	" 2nd	2/Lt De Longueuil wounded.	
"	" 3rd		

(73989) W4141—463. 400,000. 9/14. H.&J.Ltd. Forms/C. 2118/10.

13th Bde.
5th Div.

2nd K. O. Y. L. I.

JULY.

1 9 1 5.

Army Form C. 2118.

Instructions regarding War Diaries and Intelligence Summaries are contained in F. S. Regs., Part II. and the Staff Manual respectively. Title pages will be prepared in manuscript.

WAR DIARY
or
INTELLIGENCE SUMMARY.
(*Erase heading not required.*)

Place	Date	Hour	Summary of Events and Information	Remarks and references to Appendices
St. Eloi Defences	July	1st	on the whole a quiet time — occasional burst of Shelling on both sides only causing few casualties on our side. Mining & Countermining going on continuously generally in our favour.	
— " —		2nd	– Spr [illegible] Longreuil wounded –	
— " —		3rd		
— " —				
			Note/ The above has been copied from previous War Diary	

T2134. Wt. W708—776. 500000. 4/15. Sir J. C. & L.

Army Form C. 2118.

Instructions regarding War Diaries and Intelligence Summaries are contained in F.S. Regs., Part II. and the Staff Manual respectively. Title pages will be prepared in manuscript.

WAR DIARY
or
~~INTELLIGENCE SUMMARY.~~

(*Erase heading not required.*)

Hour, Date, Place		Summary of Events and Information	Remarks and references to Appendices
St ELOI Defences to Dickebush Huts.	July 4th	Relieved at 11.30 P.m. by West Riding Regt & marched back to Huts. 2/Lt Weiss rejoined his own unit. (R Berkshire Regt)	[initials]
Dickebush Huts	-"- 5th	In Huts resting. Capts Mallinson & Agg (1st Bn) visited us also Lt Col R.E. Boulton & Major Rigg (6th Bn). 2/Lt N.E. LEE attached to Mining Coy R.E.	[initials]
-"-	-"- 6th	In Huts Resting. 2/Lt Whitworth joined Battn.	[initials]
Dickebush Huts to Trenches at St ELOI	-"- 7th	Marched at 8 P.m. & relieved West Kent Regt.	[initials]
Trenches at St ELOI	-"- 8th	Things very quiet.	
-"-	-"- 9th	-"- 2/Lt P. Gurney wounded.	
-"-	-"- 10th	At 3.30 a.m. we exploded 3 Mines very successfully. One under a House which formed a German Snipers post. The Second near "The Mound" & the third under the German Trench North of The Mound. The last mine destroyed 60 x of the German Trench & the Germans running out of this trench were dealt with by our Machine Guns. Major Ellis went down Sick.	[initials]
-"-	-"- 11th	The Enemy heavily shelled our Trenches with High Explosives & Shrapnel from 4.30 a.m. to 6 a.m. also using a large Minenwerfer & Several Small ones. Damage not very Considerable. Casualties 3 Killed & 15 wounded. We were lucky in not having had more. This was probably a retaliation for blowing them up yesterday.	[initials]
-"-	12th	Quiet Day. 2/Lt Skidmore joined Battn.	

(73989) W4141—463. 400,000. 9/14. H.&J.Ltd. Forms/C. 2118/10.

Instructions regarding War Diaries and Intelligence Summaries are contained in F. S. Regs., Part II. and the Staff Manual respectively. Title pages will be prepared in manuscript.

WAR DIARY
or
INTELLIGENCE SUMMARY.
(*Erase heading not required.*)

Army Form C. 2118.

Hour, Date, Place		Summary of Events and Information	Remarks and references to Appendices
Trenches St Eloi to Dickebush Huts.	July 13th	Relieved by West Ridings at 12 MN & retired to Dickebush Huts. Col Walker 13th Hampshire Regt attached for instruction. 2/Lt Wood joined Batt.	[initials]
Dickebush Huts	—"— 14th	Resting. C Coy out digging all night. 5th Div transferred from 2nd to 10th Corps.	
—"—	—"— 15th	—"— D —"— - Draft of 50 R&F [illegible]. 2/Lt Heslop joined Batt.	[initials]
To St Eloi Trenches.	—"— 16th	Marched at 8 P.m. & relieved West Kents. ~~[illegible]~~	
St Eloi Trenches.	—"— 17th	At 2.45 a.m. the Enemy exploded a mine about 15 yards in front of the parapet of Q1 trench which was occupied at the time by C Coy (Capt Buckle). The mine went up with terrific force exploding under the Pavé Road & a ruined House. About 80x of Q1 Trench was demolished & the occupants buried. Only 5 men of No 12 Platoon survived. Falling Pavé Stones & bricks which were hurled 200 feet in the air caused many casualties in R2 & R3 Trenches (vide attached maps). The Enemy shelled & Trench Mortared these Trenches heavily for about 1 hour after the Explosion but did not attack. Our Casualties amounted to 111 (29 Killed & 82 wounded). No Officers hit. C Coy in Q1 suffered most losing 78 NCOs & men. B Coy (Capt Littledale) in R2 & R3 losing 33 NCOs & men. These two Coys behaved with great gallantry under trying circumstances, what was left of them getting up over the Parapet & opening rapid fire on the German Trenches & thereby frustrating any chance of the Enemy trying to attack Q1 Trench. The demoralizing effect of a Mine Explosion followed by a heavy bombardment might easily have caused unsteady troops to evacuate the undamaged portions of Q1 & R2 & R3 Trenches with disastrous results. After the Bombardment ceased B & C Coys spent the rest of the day in [illegible] dead & wounded & started work on the repair of their trenches. A Coy in reserve under Capt Evans Smith relieved C Coy at night in Q1 & carried on work in repairing the Trench & in 48 Hours the line was practically restored which reflected great credit on all these Companies.	[initials]

(73989) W4141—463. 400,000. 9/14. H.&J.Ltd. Forms/C. 2118/10.

Instructions regarding War Diaries and Intelligence Summaries are contained in F. S. Regs., Part II. and the Staff Manual respectively. Title pages will be prepared in manuscript.

WAR DIARY
or
INTELLIGENCE SUMMARY.
(*Erase heading not required.*)

Army Form C. 2118.

Hour, Date, Place		Summary of Events and Information	Remarks and references to Appendices
St ELOI Trenches	July 18th	at 8 a.m. our artillery bombarded the German line in retaliation for their mine explosion of 17th. There was consequently a fair by lively shell fire on both sides throughout the day with the result that our Battn Store of Tools Trench Stores Sandbags etc was set fire to & demolished. The German Parapet was however knocked down in several places. The 29 men killed were buried in our Cemetery in VOORMEZEELE.	
St ELOI Trenches	—"— 19th	Everything quiet again in the Sector.	
—"—	—"— 20th	Received orders that the 5th Divn were to be withdrawn from 2nd Corps & from 2nd Army to form part of a new 3rd Army 10th Corps. Officers of the Wiltshire Regt 7th Brigade 3rd Divn came to see the trenches.	
St Eloi Trenches & ROSEN HILL Camp near. Zevecoten.	—"— 21st	Correspondents of Morning Post & Daily Mail visited our trenches. Relieved by Wiltshire Regt (7th Bn) at 12.30 a.m. & marched to ROSENHILL CAMP.	
Rosen Hill Camp to STEENVOORDE.	22nd	Marched from ROSENHILL Camp via BOESCHEPE-GODEWAERSVELDE to STEENVOORDE (12½ Miles) - Marched off at 8 p.m. but got badly hung up owing to Bad roads & heavy rain. The Transport of Units in front of us keeping us back. We were consequently 2 hours late in arriving at BOESCHEPE & did not reach STEENVOORDE until 4.30 a.m. 23rd. Lt & Q.M. A.E. Bentham joined Battn on 23rd inst.	
STEENVOORDE.	23rd	At STEENVOORDE where 5th Divn are assembling prior to moving South to join New 3rd Army 10th Corps. Battn Billeted in Farms in a widely extended area but very comfortable.	
—"—	24th	Billets at STEENVOORDE.	
—"—	25th	—"—	
—"—	26th	13th Infty Brigade was inspected by Genl Sir H Plumer commanding 2nd Army who after his inspection made a farewell address to the Brigade as follows:- Draft of 90 R&F joined Battn.	

(73989) W4141—463. 400,000. 9/14. H.&J.Ltd. Forms/C. 2118/10.

Instructions regarding War Diaries and Intelligence Summaries are contained in F. S. Regs., Part II. and the Staff Manual respectively. Title pages will be prepared in manuscript.

WAR DIARY
or
INTELLIGENCE SUMMARY.

(*Erase heading not required.*)

Army Form C. 2118.

Hour, Date, Place	Summary of Events and Information	Remarks and references to Appendices
	Genl Wanless O'Gowan, Officers NCOs & men of 13th Infty Bde. I should not have asked you to come here today, as it is only 2 months ago since I spoke to you & congratulated you on your work in those most trying times in most difficult positions in the YPRES SALIENT, except for the fact that you are leaving the 2nd Corps & the 2nd Army which I have the honour to command. In saying Goodbye I wish to express to all Ranks my personal thanks for the splendid work done by this Brigade. I cannot add anything to what was said to you by the Commander-in-Chief & Genl Sir Horace Smith-Dorrien, but for the benefit of those of you who were not present on those occasions I will say a few words to you on the part you played in the defence of YPRES. I can assure you that the C-in-C thoroughly realizes the part played by the 13th Infy Bde in the YPRES SALIENT, although in his dispatches it is impossible & often inadvisable to mention all Brigades by name. Three separate tasks were allotted to different forces in different parts of the Salient. Through no ~~[illegible]~~ fault of our allies, the retirement on the left of the Canadians N of YPRES placed our line in a very precarious position at the point of the Salient & it became necessary for one section, I refer now to the 27th & 28th Divisions, to fall back to a freshly prepared line. ~~[illegible]~~ The task allotted to another section was to hold on to this position at all costs, & to you was allotted what may have appeared a useless & wasteful task in making attacks where casualties were taken & no apparent object was gained. I can however assure you that this was not so, for if you had not delivered those attacks at the exact moment you did & carried them out successfully it would have been impossible for the 27th & 28th Divns to withdraw at our own time to the new positions prepared for them.	

(73989) W4141—463. 400,000. 9/14. H.&J.Ltd. Forms/C. 2118/10.

Instructions regarding War Diaries and Intelligence Summaries are contained in F.S. Regs., Part II. and the Staff Manual respectively. Title pages will be prepared in manuscript.

WAR DIARY
or
INTELLIGENCE SUMMARY.
(Erase heading not required.)

Army Form C. 2118.

Hour, Date, Place	Summary of Events and Information	Remarks and references to Appendices
	as I say the splendid part played by the 13th Infty Bde was recognized by the C in C who came himself & thanked you personally both for your work at Hill 60 & also for the help you rendered to the Canadians when you went to join them.	
	I wish to thank all ranks for the magnificent way you have carried out any operation you have been called upon to perform during the time you have been under my command. You are now leaving a part of the line which when you took it over was far from satisfactory. I will not say it is perfect now as faults can always be found but I will say that by your hard work you have handed it over in a very much better & stronger state than when you took it over.	History
	You are now leaving the 2nd Army & 2nd Corps to form the nucleus of a new 10th Corps & 3rd Army & in going so take over great responsibilities as you will be, as far as this campaign is concerned the veterans of the Corps. The other newer Divisions will all look to you for guidance & I am sure you will set them a high standard & keep up the reputation that you have always held.	
	I might say that I have a personal interest in the 5th Division which I commanded in peace time & where ever you go I will always think of you.	
	Now in conclusion I wish to say that you can always look back with pride on the part that you have played in the defence of YPRES. You have lost friends & you have had some hard work & hard fighting, but no matter what you have done before or what you may do in the future, your work at YPRES will always rank with the best in the army"	

Army Form C. 2118.

WAR DIARY
or
INTELLIGENCE SUMMARY.
(Erase heading not required.)

Instructions regarding War Diaries and Intelligence Summaries are contained in F. S. Regs., Part II. and the Staff Manual respectively. Title pages will be prepared in manuscript.

Place	Date	Hour	Summary of Events and Information	Remarks and references to Appendices
STEENVOORDE	July 27th		In Billets. Held our Annual Minden Sports in the Fields near our Battn. H.Q. A most successful meeting & excellent entries. Considering the conditions (it's a somewhat rough course & only Ammn. Boots to run in) the times were very good. Programme & results attached.	[illegible]
—"—	" 28th		In Billets.	
—"—	" 29th		—"— .	
—"—	" 30th		—"— .	
STEENVOORDE to LA NEUVILLE.	" 31st		Marched from Billets at 5 a.m. to GODWAERSVELDE Railway Station where the Battn. entrained at 6.33 a.m. & proceeded via HAZEBROUCK & ST OMER to CALAIS where we halted for 1 hour. From there we went via BOULOGNE to ABBEVILLE where we halted for 1½ hours & proceeded to AMIENS where we arrived at 6.23 P.M. From there we ~~[illegible]~~ CORBIE where we detrained & marched to Billets in LA NEUVILLE. 2/Lts Davies & McDougall joined Battn.	[illegible]

D. D. & L., London, E.C.
(10340) Wt W5300/P713 750,000 3/18 E 2688 Forms C/2118/16.

13th Bde.

5th Div.

2nd K. O. Y. L. I.

AUGUST.

1 9 1 5

Instructions regarding War Diaries and Intelligence Summaries are contained in F. S. Regs., Part II. and the Staff Manual respectively. Title pages will be prepared in manuscript.

WAR DIARY
or
INTELLIGENCE SUMMARY.
(Erase heading not required.)

2 K.O.Y.L.I

Army Form C. 2118.

Place	Date	Hour	Summary of Events and Information	Remarks and references to Appendices
AT LA NEUVILLE.	Minden Day.		In Billets at LA NEUVILLE. The men picked roses from the gardens in the neighbourhood + wore them as usual.	[illegible]
LA NEUVILLE.	August 2nd		In Billets.	
LA NEUVILLE TO RIBEMONT.	" 3rd		Marched at 11 a.m. & reached RIBEMONT at 1 P.M. At 3.30 P.M. the Brigade paraded for inspection in Marching Order by Genl MUNRO Commanding 3rd Army. After Parade we went into Billets.	[illegible]
RIBEMONT to BRONFRAY.	" 4th		Marched via MERICOURT - BRAY to BRONFRAY FARM (12 miles). Started at 7.30 P.M. & halted for Teas near BRAY. Got much delayed by French Regts crossing our front. Reached BRONFRAY FARM at 12.30 a.m. where we took over from the French. BRONFRAY FARM forms a strong defended post known as the Bridge Head of BRAY as it covers the Bridge over the SOMME at BRAY.	[illegible]

(73989) W4141—463. 400,000. 9/14. H.&J.Ltd. Forms/C. 2118/10.

T2134. Wt. W708—776. 500000. 4/15. Sir J. C. & S.

Instructions regarding War Diaries and Intelligence Summaries are contained in F. S. Regs., Part II. and the Staff Manual respectively. Title pages will be prepared in manuscript.

WAR DIARY
or
INTELLIGENCE SUMMARY.
(*Erase heading not required.*)

Army Form C. 2118.

Hour, Date, Place		Summary of Events and Information	Remarks and references to Appendices
BRONFAY FARM	August 5th	In Brigade reserve at BRONFAY - French gradually disappearing - A + D Coys moved into wood East of BILLON FARM.	
— " —	— " — 6th	Brigade Reserve. B Coy moved into Dugouts S.W. of BRONFRAY	
— " —	— " — 7th	— " —	
— " —	— " — 8th	— " — Lt Hicks rejoined Battn + Capt Littledale assumed duties of 2nd in Command.	
— " —	— " — 9th	— " —	
— " —	— " — 10th	— " —	
— " —	— " — 11th	— " —	
— " —	— " — 12th	— " —	
— " —	— " — 13th	— " —	
— " —	— " — 14th	— " —	
Bronfray to Trenches at Carnoy	— " — 15th	Marched to Trenches at CARNOY at 8.30 p.m. + relieved West Kent Regt.	
Trenches at CARNOY	— " — 16th	Everything very quiet in the Sector.	
— " —	— " — 17th	— " —	
— " —	— " — 18th	Capt Littledale left to join 6th Battn in exchange with Capt E.A. Rigg.	
— " —	— " — 19th	Trenches at CARNOY.	
— " —	— " — 20th	— " — B: Genl R. Wanless O'Gowan gave up command of the 13th Infy Bde being succeeded by B: Genl MAYNARD.	
— " —	— " — 21st	— " —	
— " —	— " — 22nd	— " — A Coy on our left was relieved by 1 Coy Bn Suffolks + D Coy relieved 1 Coy of 9th QVR on our right - the Battn thus	
— " —	— " — 23rd	— " — "sideslipped" to its right.	
Trenches to BRONFRAY Fm.	— " — 24th	Relieved by West Kents at 11 p.m. + retired to reserve at BRONFRAY. Capt E.A. Rigg joined Battn on exchange with Capt Littledale.	
BRONFRAY.	— " — 25th	In reserve at BRONFRAY - large working parties out each night on Communication Trenches.	
— " —	— " — 26th		
— " —	— " — 27th		
— " —	— " — 28th		
— " —	— " — 29th		
— " —	— " — 30th		
— " —	— " — 31st		

(73989) W4141—463. 400,000. 9/14. H.&J.Ltd. Forms/C. 2118/10.

13th Bde.

5th Div.

2nd K. O. Y. L. I.

SEPTEMBER.

1 9 1 5

Instructions regarding War Diaries and Intelligence Summaries are contained in F. S. Regs., Part II. and the Staff Manual respectively. Title pages will be prepared in manuscript.

WAR DIARY
or
INTELLIGENCE SUMMARY.
(*Erase heading not required.*)

Army Form C. 2118.

Hour, Date, Place		Summary of Events and Information	Remarks and references to Appendices
BRONFRAY FARM to Trenches at CARNOY.	September 1st	Moved up at 8 P.M. & relieved K.O.S.B. in B2 Sector.	
Trenches at CARNOY	2nd	Quiet Day in trenches B2 Subsector.	
—"—	3rd	We blew up a Mine in front of 50 Trench at 7.30 P.M. Extent of damage unknown.	
—"—	4th	Fairly quiet. Enemy blew up 2 mines opposite 50 Trench at 6.30 P.M. & 7.30 P.M. blowing in our listening Posts in the "Etonnoirs" vide Sketch. A certain amount of shelling followed but no damage was done. The origin of the somewhat interesting situation in the "Entonnoirs" was as follows:- The Germans originally blew up a series of mines nearer their own main trench than our own. The French, who then held our line, ran forward after the explosions & occupied the near edge of the Craters which were some 30 feet deep. Their object being to prevent the Germans from using these craters as a basis for further mining operations towards our main line. They then dug a trench along the line of craters with commn trenches back to the main line; the Germans did the same, holding the craters with listening posts only. The listening posts in places being only 7 yards apart. All the mining operations now consist in blowing in each others mine shafts & as long as the craters are held both main lines are safe.	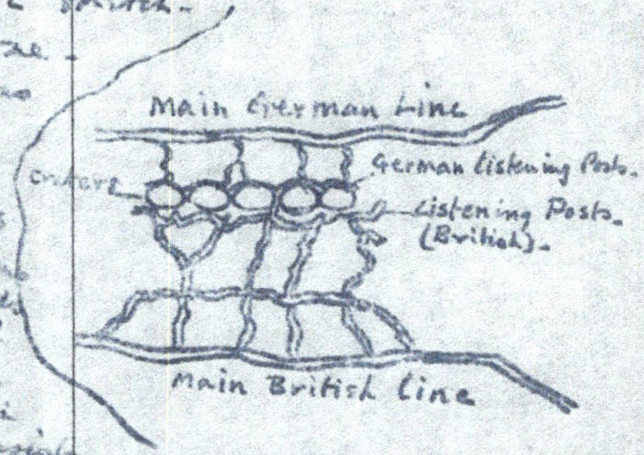
Trenches at Carnoy	5th	Quiet day in B2 Subsector. 2nd Lt Woods 3/K.O.Y.L.I. joined Battn.	
—"—	6th	—"—	
—"—	7th	—"—	
—"—	8th	—"—	
Trenches to Bray.	9th	Relieved in Trenches by K.O.S.Bs & retired to Billets in BRAY.	

(73989) W4141—463. 400,000. 9/14. H.&J.Ltd. Forms/C. 2118/10.

Instructions regarding War Diaries and Intelligence Summaries are contained in F. S. Regs., Part II. and the Staff Manual respectively. Title pages will be prepared in manuscript.

WAR DIARY
or
INTELLIGENCE SUMMARY.
(Erase heading not required.)

Army Form C. 2118.

Place	Hour, Date	Summary of Events and Information	Remarks and references to Appendices
BRAY	Sept 10th	In Billets at Bray - Digging Parties out all ~~day~~ night on Second line defences.	
—"—	—"— 11th		
—"—	—"— 12th	—"— Lt Ryan 1st/6th Black Watch joined for instruction as Adjt.	
—"—	—"— 13th	—"— Draft of 27 R.F. joined Battn.	
—"—	—"— 14th	—"— Major CHUTE 10th R.I.R. and Major PRATT 10th R. Irish Fusiliers.	
—"—	—"— 15th	attached for 2 days for instruction.	
—"—	—"— 16th	—"—	
To Trenches at CARNOY.	—"— 17th	Marched at 6.30 P.M. to Trenches at CARNOY and relieved the K.O.S.B.s in B2 Subsector.	
Trenches at CARNOY	—"— 18th	Quiet Day.	
—"—	—"— 19th	—"—	
—"—	—"— 20th	—"—	
—"—	—"— 21st	Conference at B2 Subsector H.Q. with Br Genl & all C.O.s at which he informed us that the 13th Infy Bde was to be withdrawn from the line to prepare for an attack on a sector of the German line E of MAMETZ in the event of the Germans weakening their line as a result of the forthcoming offensive by the French in Champagne & British (1st Army) near La BASSEE & the French 10th Corps near SOUCHEZ. The B.G.C 15th Infy Bde & other officers came round the trenches to see them.	
—"—	—"— 22nd	Quiet Day in Trenches. Officers of Dorsets & Cheshire Regt came round the trenches.	
Trenches to BRAY	—"— 23rd	Relieved at 10.30 P.M. by Dorsets & 1 Coy of Cheshire Regt & retired to Bray, leaving 400 Men to dig till dawn.	
BRAY.	24th	at BRAY. Capt Gharcut joined the Battn.	
—"—	25th	—"— all officers out reconnoitring the German Trenches in front of B3 subsector. Capt de R. Martin joined the Battn	

(73989) W4141—463. 400,000. 9/14. H.&J.Ltd. Forms/C. 2118/10.

Army Form C. 2118.

Instructions regarding War Diaries and Intelligence Summaries are contained in F.S. Regs., Part II. and the Staff Manual respectively. Title pages will be prepared in manuscript.

WAR DIARY
or
INTELLIGENCE SUMMARY.
(Erase heading not required.)

Hour, Date, Place		Summary of Events and Information	Remarks and references to Appendices
BRAY	Sept 26th	Brigade practised the assault during the afternoon.	[illegible]
—"—	—"— 27th	In Bray. } Large digging & Mining parties out all night	
—"—	—"— 28th	—"— } & day.	
—"—	—"— 29th	—"—	
—"—	—"— 30th	—"— K.O.S.B. & K.O.Y.L.I. marched past the Army Commander in ETINEHEM.	[illegible]

[illegible] Capt
Adjt [illegible] K.O.Y.L.I.

13th Bde.

5th Div.

2nd K. O. Y. L. I.

OCTOBER

1 9 1 5

Instructions regarding War Diaries and Intelligence Summaries are contained in F. S. Regs., Part II. and the Staff Manual respectively. Title pages will be prepared in manuscript.

WAR DIARY
or
INTELLIGENCE SUMMARY.
(Erase heading not required.)

Army Form C. 2118.

Place	Hour, Date 1915	Summary of Events and Information	Remarks and references to Appendices
BRAY.	October 1st	at BRAY. Large digging & mining Parties out Day & Night. Heard more or less definitely that the 13th Bde would not make their attack as the Enemy are not apparently weakening their line on this front with a view to general retirement.	[initials]
BRAY & Bronfray.	-"- 2nd	13th Bde relieved 15th Bde in Carnoy Sectors. A Coy moved up to BILLON WOOD & D Coy to BRONFRAY. B & C Coys & Bn HQ. remained in BRAY. Large working & Mining parties out.	[initials]
BRAY & BRONFRAY.	3rd 4th 5th 6th 7th	Large Mining & working Parties out by day & Night. Draft of 13 R+F joined Battn.	[initials]
BRONFRAY.	8th	B & C Coys & Bn HQ moved to BRONFRAY & BILLON at 6 P.M. & relieved the 9th Glosters.	[initials]
BRONFRAY & BILLON.	9th	At BILLON & BRONFRAY.	
Trenches at CARNOY.	10th	Moved to Trenches & relieved the K.O.S.B.s at 8 P.M.	[initials]
Trenches at	11th	Quiet Day.	[initials]

Instructions regarding War Diaries and Intelligence Summaries are contained in F. S. Regs., Part II. and the Staff Manual respectively. Title pages will be prepared in manuscript.

WAR DIARY
or
INTELLIGENCE SUMMARY.
(*Erase heading not required.*)

Army Form C. 2118.

Hour, Date, Place		Summary of Events and Information	Remarks and references to Appendices
Trenches at CARNOY.	Oct 12th	Everything very quiet	[initials]
—"—	" 13th.	—"—	[initials]
To BRAY.	" 14th	Relieved by 10th Black Watch at 10 P.M. who took over our Sector for instruction – at 8.30 P.M. a Mine exploded on our left which was followed by a lot of Rifle – shell fire.	[initials]
To SAILLY LORETTE	" 15th.	The Battn retired to SAILLY LORETTE marching from BRAY at 6 P.M. leaving behind the following Officers to be attached to 11th Scottish Rifles to instruct them in Trench work. Capt M.F. Day. 2nd Lt Gask. Lts Sales-Wells. Davies. Stewart. A Draft of 30 R&F joined Battn.	[initials]
at SAILLY LORETTE.	" 16th, " 17th, " 18th, " 19th, " 20th	In Billets at SAILLY LORETTE. Two Companies out each day digging a fourth line near ETINHEM. Lt Col Wm. Withycombe left the Battn to take Command of 107th Infty Brigade – 36th Division.	[initials] [initials]
To BRAY.	" 21st	Battn marched to Bray from SAILLY LORETTE.	
Bray	" 22nd, " 23rd, " 24th, " 25th	Billets in Bray. Large working Parties out by day & night.	[initials]
BRAY to Trenches at CARNOY	" 26th	Battn marched from BRAY at 4.45 P.M. & relieved K.O.S.B. in trenches at CARNOY.	[initials]
Trenches at CARNOY	" 27th	Everything very quiet in the Sector. Trenches in a bad state owing to rain.	[initials]

Instructions regarding War Diaries and Intelligence Summaries are contained in F. S. Regs., Part II. and the Staff Manual respectively. Title pages will be prepared in manuscript.

WAR DIARY
or
INTELLIGENCE SUMMARY.
(*Erase heading not required.*)

Army Form C. 2118.

Hour, Date, Place		Summary of Events and Information	Remarks and references to Appendices
Trenches at Carnoy	Oct 28th	At 5 am. the Germans exploded a mine in the Entonnoirs blowing in our left listening Post but otherwise doing themselves more harm than us. No Casualties resulted although the Germans shelled our trenches after the explosion. One more crater hole has been added to the line of Entonnoirs necessitating the running out of another listening Post to occupy our edge of it.	[initials]
—"—	29th	Increased artillery activity chiefly on our Part otherwise	
—"—	30th	everything very quiet. 18 Rnf joined Battn under 2/Lt	[initials]
—"—	31st	Jennings 10th KOYLI. This officer returned to Entrenching Bn.	

[signature] Capt
2/KOYLI

13th Bde.

5th Div.

2nd K. O. Y. L. I.

....

1 9 1 5

13th Bde.
5th Div.

2nd K. O. Y. L. I.

NOVEMBER.

1915

Instructions regarding War Diaries and Intelligence Summaries are contained in F. S. Regs., Part II. and the Staff Manual respectively. Title pages will be prepared in manuscript.

WAR DIARY
or
INTELLIGENCE SUMMARY.
(Erase heading not required.)

2nd Battn: K.O.Y.L.I.

Army Form C. 2118.

Hour, Date, Place		Summary of Events and Information	Remarks and references to Appendices
Trenches at CARNOY – November	1st	Relieved by K.O.S.B. Marched to dug-outs, B Coy + H.Q.rs at BRONFAY, A.C.D Coys. in BILLON WOOD.	[illegible]
BRONFAY and BILLON WOOD	Nov. 2nd, 3rd, 4th, 5th, 6th	Large working parties digging in CARNOY trenches.	[illegible]
Trenches at CARNOY	7th	Relieved K.O.S.B. in trenches which are getting in a very bad state owing to the weather.	
"	8th, 9th	Quiet days. 2/Lt Constable 3/5th Yorks L.I. joined for duty with [illegible]. Capt. Day left to take up [illegible] of 3rd Army Cadet School	[illegible]
	10th	Heavy rain. Crater sector parapets falling in – support line almost invisible.	
"	11th	Weather still bad. Situation quiet.	[illegible]
"	12th	Enemy artillery more active.	
"	13th	Relieved by K.O.S.B. at 7.30 pm. Returned to Billets at BRAY.	
BRAY	14th	Rest	
"	15th, 16th	Snowed both days. 100 men digging in CARNOY trenches.	
"	17th, 18th	180 men on fatigue at CARNOY and BRONFAY. 2/Lt Lee transferred to 253rd Tunnelling Coy. & struck off strength. Relieved K.O.S.B. in trenches at 7.30 pm.	[illegible]
"	19th	A few shells fell in Bray last night but none exploded.	[illegible]
Trenches at CARNOY	20th	Enemy's artillery more active – shelled our right trenches & CARNOY	[illegible]
"	21st	C.S. Major GOODACRE killed and 1 man wounded putting out wire	[illegible]
"	22nd	Sergt. King wounded – heavy mist – strong parties put out by day wiring.	[illegible]
"	23rd	Enemy's artillery active searching for machine guns in our right sector	[illegible]
"	24th	Our artillery active; enemy replied with grenades on centre & left sectors	[illegible]
"	24th	Enemy blew up mine at 6.30 am. trying to destroy our saps. No casualties. Enemy's artillery, trench mortars & grenades very active but no casualties. Captain Day appointed Bde. Major 107th Brigade.	[illegible]

(73989) W4141—463. 400,000. 9/14. H.&J.Ltd. Forms/C. 2118/10.

Instructions regarding War Diaries and Intelligence Summaries are contained in F. S. Regs., Part II. and the Staff Manual respectively. Title pages will be prepared in manuscript.

WAR ~~DIARY~~

or

INTELLIGENCE SUMMARY.

(*Erase heading not required.*)

Army Form C. 2118.

2nd Battn: K.O.Y.L.I.

Hour, Date, Place		Summary of Events and Information	Remarks and references to Appendices
Trenches at CARNOY	Nov: 25th	Enemy shelled CARNOY and our right trenches. Relieved in evening by K.O.S.B. A Coy to BRONFAY FARM with H.Q.rs. B.C.D Coys to BILLON WOOD.	[illegible]
	" 26th	Snow.	[illegible]
BRONFAY and BILLON	" 27	Snow — very cold — Battn: furnishing very heavy fatigues	[illegible]
	" 28	At rest in Bronfay & Billon — about 3 Companies on fatigue every day.	
—"—	" 29		
	" 30	Enemy shelled just S. of Bronfay farm — about 3 heavy shells came over — [illegible] 200 yards of the farm.	[illegible]

[illegible] 9/1/[illegible]

Report by Intelligence Officer
2/KOYLI 10/11/15

The night was fairly quiet
our patrols went out but could not
gain any information.
Two or three sentries in the
centre sector reported that a
German patrol was seen about
11 30, ~~and~~ on firing at them
they went away.
The Germans had a Machine
Gun firing on 50 trench
but I was unable to locate it.
Nothing else to report

G A Gamble 2Lt
2/KOYLI

Report by Intelligence Officer
2/ KOYLI

8/11

The night was very quiet
The enemy did a certain amount of
work behind the craters.
Several large fires have been seen
to day, most of them being in their
support trenches.
Nothing else to report.

[illegible] 2Lt
2/ KOYLI

8/11/15.

Report by Intelligence Officer
2/KOYLI. 11-11-15

The night was very quiet.
During the afternoon of the 10th a german was seen wearing khaki uniform and one of our service caps.

This morning the enemy was seen using the road between MONTAUBAN and the BRIQUERIES. Four men were seen to walk down the road, and then a cyclist was seen just where the railway crosses the road at ~~[illegible]~~ A 3 C 8.2

A large column of smoke was seen rising from this point. The road appeared to have been used a great deal, probably for bringing up rations. It is suggested that some head quarters are at this point.

Sd. G.A. Gamble 2/Lt.
2/KOYLI

Report by Intelligence Officer
7/KOYLI 12.11.15

The enemy's trenches opposite 42 trench were bombed by us. The damage done is not known.

Our machine guns were fired up till 12.30 am. and evidently caused some annoyance to the enemy for they tried to hit one gun with bombs. With this exception the enemy was exceedingly quiet.

At 11.30 am a large column of smoke was seen rising from the place reported yesterday i.e. A 3 c 8.2. This point is where the dug-outs for the H.Q. of the unit in the trenches are probably situated

Sd. G.A. Lamble 2/Lt.
7/KOYLI

Report by Intelligence Offr
2/KOYLI 13/11/15

1 Situation

Yesterday was very quiet not a sign of any movement anywhere. Last night and this morning were also very quiet.
I think the enemy must be having the same trouble with his trenches as we are, for he is not so keen on sniping as he used to be.

Nothing else to report

G.A. Gamble 2Lt
2/KOYLI

Report by Intelligence officer
2nd K.O.Y.L.I.

Sub. Sector B2 20/11/15.

I The night passed quietly. There was a bright moon and as usual on moonlight nights less sniping than usual.

II At 8.50 p.m. last night horse transport was heard on the road near point A 3 C 9/3 ref 1/10.000.

III At about 7 p.m. a German machine gun was firing bursts of about 20 rounds at a time for about a quarter of an hour at the sandbags in 42 support trench. It would appear that the enemy were searching for the light railway behind the Q.V.R's sector.

20/11

IV At about 11.30 a.m. to-day two German officers were seen ~~standing~~ walking about in the bushes & ~~to~~ near point A3C 9/3 ref $\frac{1}{10,000}$ - They were dressed in long light blue double-breasted frock coats and were tall. They wore no hats and had their hands in their pockets. Apparently there is a Headquarters near this point. It has been suspected before from previous observations

V The enemy's listening post opposite 42 trench is being steel-lined probably with a view to converting it into a trench mortar or minnenwerfer emplacement.

In front of this post the enemy has been copying our idea by putting out balls of wire similar to ours.

VI Opposite 52 Trench the enemy has recently put up more

barbed wire – apparently of the "knife rest" pattern.

G.H. Kent Captain
I.O. 2/K.O.Y.L.I.

20/11/15.

Intelligence Report
by I.O. 2/K.O.Y.L.I.

Sub-Sector B2 21/11/15.

I About 7 p.m. last night a loud explosion was heard in the german trenches opposite 41 trench and a large column of black smoke rose in the air. It is thought that a ~~[illegible]~~ a "Sausage" must have exploded accidentally. This is borne out by some of the Q.V.R who state that they saw a fuze burning for some seconds before the explosion took place.

II One of our sentries in 42 trench was looking through a periscope when he observed a large periscope in the german advanced post opposite. He fired at it and smashed it to atoms.

III The enemy showed greater activity last night than usual. There was much more sniping. This seems to ~~point~~ to indicate a relief having taken place.

IV The OC West Bomb Battery in 42 trench reports that 3 Germans were seen in their advanced post opposite 42 trench apparently attending to a wounded man. A bomb was fired and dropped right into the post and must have caused considerable damage.

V As stated in my report of yesterday this advanced post opposite 42 trench is being steel lined and strengthened – It is probable that the enemy are building a minnenwerfer emplacement to reply to our West Bomb thrower. This is further borne out by the fact that it was in this neighbourhood that the explosion occurred as reported in para I of this report. Possibly sausages were being carried up to this point. It is suggested that the artillery be asked to shell this spot with high explosive.

VI A german machine gun was again firing this evening from some point away on our right flank (approximately near A 9 b 3/6 ref 1/10,000) and splitting the sandbags in 42 Support trench – traversing along the parapet.

G.H. Kent Captain

21/11/15 1.0 2/K.O.Y.L.I.

Report by Intelligence Officer
2/K.O.Y.L.I.

Sub Sector B2 22/11/15

I. Last night and to-day have been very quiet. There has been a thick fog all day and observation has been impossible.

II About 2.30 p.m. yesterday a german was seen in the advanced post opposite 42 trench. He showed a head & shoulders above the parapet. He was wearing a round cap and overcoat. A steady aim was taken at him and he was seen to drop and did not appear again.

III Our wiring party last night in front of 51 trench saw a german patrol near the Barricade. Our party came in and rapid fire was opened in the direction the patrol was seen. The result of the fire could not be seen but the patrol were not seen any more.

IV Some of our men who were out examining our wire in front of 47 and 48 trenches this afternoon saw figures of Germans looming up through the fog opposite. Our party returned to the trench and opened rapid fire.

V A similar episode occurred in front of 51 trench where our wiring party also saw two Germans and opened fire on them. This party of ours also found five French corpses beyond the barricade beside the Montauban road. They were in an advanced stage of decomposition. They were in full marching order. Beside them was a rifle with a round in the breech.

VI The West Bomb Battery fired 26 rounds to-day. One was seen to fall right into a German advanced post and moans were heard.

22/11/15

G.H. Kent Captain
I.O. 2/K.O.Y.L.I.

Report by Intelligence Officer
2/K.O.Y.L.I.

Left Sector B2 23.11.15

I Last night and most of to-day there has been thick mist and observation has been difficult.

II About 11 p.m. last night a german working party was seen in front of our left listening post in the craters.
Rapid fire was opened on them and they were dispersed.
Another working party was ~~seen~~ heard about 10 p.m. last night in front of 47 & 48 trenches.
Rapid fire was opened in the direction of the noise.

- About 12 noon to-day the 52nd Battery R.F.A. fired 19 shrapnel and 12 H.E. shells at german advanced post in front of 42 trench (referred to in previous reports). No direct hit was obtained but the enemy was probably caused a good deal of annoyance as he replied with rifle grenades.

III This morning one german was seen in the open in front of 43 trench walking about in the mist. He was fired at & it is believed he was hit. A patrol is going out to-night to see if he can be found.

IV A German band was heard playing to-day near MONTAUBAN about 12.30 p.m. and again at 4 p.m. ~~about 12.30 p.m.~~ Each time the band was heard a motor car was also heard on the MONTAUBAN ROAD.

G.H. Kent Captain

23.11.15 I.O. 2nd KOYLI

Report by Intelligence Officer
2/K.O.Y.L.I.

Sub Sector B2 24/11/15

I Our machine guns fired last night at intervals on roads near Montauban and point A3C93. About 6 p.m. the enemy replied with "whizz bangs" and guns of larger calibre.
About 6 p.m. last night heavy transport was heard on roads near Montauban. The artillery were informed and opened fire on the roads. The enemy replied by shelling Maricourt.

II A working party was seen last night off L9 (our left listening post on edge of Aldans) We opened fire with rifles and machine guns. Apparently the enemy are digging a new trench or post there as they have been seen working in the same place several times recently.

III About 3 trucks were seen standing on the railway at A4 a 3/5 this morning.

IV This morning our artillery fired 27 H.E. shell at enemy advanced post opposite 42 trench. The enemy replied several hours later with a few "whizz-bangs".

V At 1 p.m. to-day 30 rifle grenades fell near 47 trench. Two hit the parapet and the remainder fell behind the parados. 47 trench is quite 300 yards from the german lines and this is the first time rifle grenades have fallen near it. The germans must have some new machine for firing them which can fire at longer ranges.

24.11.15

G. H. Kent Captain
I.O. 2/KOYLI

Report by Intelligence Officer
2/K.O.Y.L.I.

Sub Sector B2 25/11/15

I Last night the enemy was very active with rifle grenades and trench mortars all along our front. One bomb which failed to explode was fetched in by the regiment on our left and is reported to be larger and of a different type to any seen before.

II The enemy exploded a mine at 5.30 a.m. this morning in front of our listening posts but no damage was done.

III There is no doubt now that the enemy have a new trench or sap head, immediately opposite 3 our left listening post (L9). This has been suspected for some days as they have been seen working ~~last~~ there.

IV We threw some handgrenades last night from listening post No 6 in front of 50 trench. Squeals were heard like those of a goat.

V A large German bi-plane flew over CARNOY at 9.50 a.m. this morning. It turned round just over CARNOY and went back towards German lines. It looked very new and in the distance very like ~~an~~ one ~~ott~~ of our machines. It was not shelled. Later it returned flying further behind our lines and this time was heavily shelled & turned back.

8

VI The enemy fired about half a dozen large shells into CARNOY at 11 a.m. this morning.
Our artillery replied by shelling MAMETZ.

G. H. Ken[illegible] Capt.

I.O. 21 [illegible]

25/11/15

13th Bde.
5th Div.

Transferred to 97th Bde. 32nd Division 25.12.15.

2nd K. O. Y. L. I.

D E C E M B E R

1 9 1 5

To 97 Bde
32 Div

Army Form C. 2118.

Instructions regarding War Diaries and Intelligence Summaries are contained in F. S. Regs., Part II. and the Staff Manual respectively. Title pages will be prepared in manuscript.

WAR DIARY
or
INTELLIGENCE SUMMARY.
(*Erase heading not required.*)

2nd K.O.Y.L.I.

Hour, Date, Place		Summary of Events and Information	Remarks and references to Appendices
Trenches at CARNOY	Dec 1st 1915	Relieved 2/K.O.S.B. in trenches. Weather very bad. Trenches in bad state	[illegible]
— " —	2nd	Weather so bad that communication trenches almost impassable so rations are sent across the open at night. 2/Lt WILLINGTON to 7th Batt. + 2/Lt PATTERSON to 6th Batt.	[illegible]
— " —	3rd	1 man missing from patrol. Dugouts falling in: 2 men buried + killed	[illegible]
— " —	4th	Patrol under 2/Lt HESLOP went out + bombed enemy listening post opposite 42 trench	[illegible]
— " —	5th	Officers + NCO's 14/R. Warwicks came in for instruction	[illegible]
— " —	6th	One Company 14/R.W. Regt came in for instruction. Enemy very quiet.	[illegible]
— " —	7th	Relieved by 2/K.O.S.B. Batt. returned to billets in BRAY	[illegible]
BRAY	8th	2/Lts WHITE, SCOTT and TURPIN joined from 3rd Batt.	[illegible]
"	9th 10th	Very heavy fatigues	[illegible]
"	11th	Relieved K.O.S.B. in B2	[illegible]
Trenches at CARNOY	12th	At 6.45 am a German Pole belonging to 62nd Regt. gave himself up in centre sector. Trenches very bad condition – water over waist deep in centre sector.	[illegible]
— " —	13th	Quiet day; trenches still very bad	[illegible]
— " —	14th	Trenches improving slightly.	[illegible]
— " —	15th	Relieved by K.O.S.B. – Batt. retired to FROISSY HUTS	[illegible]
FROISSY HUTS	16th	Rest. Light fatigues	[illegible]
— " —	17th	Rest. Light fatigues	

Instructions regarding War Diaries and Intelligence Summaries are contained in F. S. Regs., Part II. and the Staff Manual respectively. Title pages will be prepared in manuscript.

WAR DIARY
or
INTELLIGENCE SUMMARY. 2nd KOYLI
(Erase heading not required.)

Army Form C. 2118.

Hour, Date, Place		Summary of Events and Information	Remarks and references to Appendices
FROISSY HUTS	Dec 18th	Marched to BRONFAY and BILLON Wood	[illegible]
BRONFAY and BILLON	19th	Relieved KOSB in Trenches	[illegible]
Trenches at CARNOY	20th	Quiet day. Trenches still in bad condition. 2/Lt N. [illegible] slightly wounded.	[illegible]
— " —	21st	Rain.	[illegible]
— " —	22nd	do.	[illegible]
— " —	23rd	Relieved by K.O.S.B. Battn returned to BRAY.	[illegible]
BRAY	24th	Regimental canteen opened for first time, having [illegible] S. of BRAY	[illegible]
	25th	Xmas [illegible]	
	26th	Inter company [illegible] matches. A Coy won. [illegible] Officers	[illegible]
	27th	Battn marched to FROISSY HUTS	[illegible]
FROISSY HUTS	28th	Having previously received orders that the Battn was to be transferred from 13th Brigade 5th Div to 97th Inf Bde 32nd Div. the Battn was inspected by Brig Genl L.O.W. JONES D.S.O. Comdg 13th Bde. He made a very complimentary speech. The Battn marched to SAILLY LORETTE. Lt Col RIGG went to see G.O.C. 97th Inf Bde at AVELUY. Brig Genl WITHYCOMBE CMG and Capt DAY visited the Battn	[illegible]
SAILLY LORETTE	29th	Rest.	[illegible]
ALBERT	30th	Battn marched to ALBERT en route for BOUZINCOURT. Capt O.K. BUTLER joined battn & took command of A Coy. [illegible]	[illegible]
BOUZINCOURT	31st	Battn marched to billets in BOUZINCOURT.	[illegible]

[illegible] Capt
A/Adjt 2 KOYLI

(73989) W4141—463. 400,000. 9/14. H.&J.Ltd. Forms/C. 2118/10.

5 DIVISION

13 BDE

9 BN LONDON REGT

1914 OCT – 1916 JAN

TO 56 DIV – 169 BDE

13th Brigade.

5th Division.

Disembarked HAVRE 5.11.14. Joined 13th Brigade 27.11.14.

To 56 DIV
169 Bde

9th BATTALION

THE LONDON REGIMENT

18.10.14 to 3. 1. 15.

Jan 1916

Army Form C. 2118.

Instructions regarding War Diaries and Intelligence Summaries are contained in F. S. Regs., Part II. and the Staff Manual respectively. Title pages will be prepared in manuscript.

WAR DIARY

or

~~INTELLIGENCE SUMMARY.~~

(*Erase heading not required.*)

9th (County of London) Bn. The London Regt. (Queen Victoria's Rifles).

Hour, Date, Place		Summary of Events and Information	Remarks and references to Appendices
1914			
October 18th – 29th	FLEET to EASTLEIGH	Railway duty. No diary kept.	
" 30th	WINCHESTER	Moved to Rest Camp. SOUTHAMPTON.	
" 31st to Nov 3rd	SOUTHAMPTON.	Refitting Bn. for foreign service.	
November 4th	"	Embarked on S.S. OXONIAN.	
" 5th	HAVRE.	arrived at HAVRE and marched to Rest Camp.	
" 6th	"	left for ST OMER.	
" 7th	ST OMER	Arrived ST OMER and marched to ARCQUES.	
" 8th – 18th	ARCQUES.	Training and musketry.	
" 19th	"	Moved to HAZEBROUCK.	
" 20th	HAZEBROUCK.	moved to BAILLEUL.	
" 21st to 26th	BAILLEUL	Route marching and training.	
" 27th	"	Moved to NEUVE EGLISE.	
" 29th	NEUVE EGLISE.	A and B companies in trenches.	9 (28 A)
" 30th	" "	Machine gun section in trenches.	
Dec 1st	" "	C and D Companies relieve A and B Companies in trenches.	
" 4th	" "	C " " relieved from trenches. 1 killed 1 wounded.	
" 6th	" "	Instruction by R E in making fascines.	
" 8th	" "	A Company in trenches.	
" 9th	" "	B " " , D Company digging trenches. 2 wounded.	
" 10th	" "	C " dig trenches.	
" 11th	" "	Battalion moved to DRANOUTRE.	
" 12th	DRANOUTRE.	A and B Companies relieved from trenches.	
" 14th – 15th	"	Battalion in Divisional Reserve. Bn. Hdqrs moved during day to 13th Bde Hdqrs.	
" 16th	"	Bn. occupy trenches. 1 wounded.	
" 17th – 19th	"	" " " 3 killed. 5 wounded.	
" 20th	"	Bn. relieved from trenches.	
" 22nd	"	Bn. occupy trenches near LINDENHOEK.	
" 23rd	"	Bn. relieved by 1st Devons and went into billets at ST JAN'S CAPPEL.	
" 27th	ST JAN'S CAPPEL	Instruction by R E in use of hand grenades.	

Instructions regarding War Diaries and Intelligence Summaries are contained in F. S. Regs., Part II. and the Staff Manual respectively. Title pages will be prepared in manuscript.

WAR DIARY
or
INTELLIGENCE SUMMARY.
(Erase heading not required.)

Army Form C. 2118.

Hour, Date, Place		Summary of Events and Information	Remarks and references to Appendices
Dec 29th	ST JAN'S CAPPEL	~~Instruction by RE in use of hand grenades~~ Bn move to NEUVE EGLISE	
" 30th	NEUVE EGLISE	Instruction in use of hand grenades.	
" 31st	" "	Bn occupy trenches, relieving KOYLI.	
Jan 1st – 3rd 1915	" "	" " " . Lt Fargus & 10 NCO's & men killed. 36 other ranks wounded.	

10/1/15

W. B. Shipley Lieut Col Commd
9th Co of London
(Queen Victoria's Rifles)

(9 29 6) W 3332 - 1107 100,000 10/13 H W V Forms/C. 2118/10.

13th Bde.

5th Div.

9th LONDON REGT.

JANUARY

To December

1 9 1 5

9th COUNTY OF LONDON (QUEEN VICTORIA'S RIFLES)

Instructions regarding War Diaries and Intelligence Summaries are contained in F. S. Regs., Part II. and the Staff Manual respectively. Title pages will be prepared in manuscript.

WAR DIARY
or
INTELLIGENCE SUMMARY.
(*Erase heading not required.*)

Army Form C. 2118.

Hour, Date, Place	Summary of Events and Information	Remarks and references to Appendices
January 1st 1915	Bn in trenches near WULVERGHEM. 11 killed. 31 wounded.	
" 2nd	" " " " " — 2 "	
" 3rd	Bn returned to billets at NEUVE EGLISE	
" 4th	Bn in billets.	9th London
" 5th	NEUVE EGLISE shelled about noon. 7 killed. 15 wounded. 4 [illegible].	
" 6th 10 am	Inspection of Bn G.O.C. 2nd Army Corps. Bn occupy trenches.	
" 7th, 8th & 9th	Bn in trenches. Relieved evening of 9th.	
" 10th	Bn marched to BAILLEUL.	
" 11th – 15th	Medical inspection of Bn. Short route marches &c.	
" 16th	Bn march to billets at REVETSBURG.	
" 19th – 21st	A & B Coys occupy trenches near WULVERGHEM.	
" 22nd & 23rd	C & D relieve A & B. 1 wounded.	
" 24th	C & D relieved. Bn march into billets at BAILLEUL.	
" 25th & 26th	Inspection of rifles, feet, clothing & accoutrements.	
" 27th – 30th	Orders received midnight 26th to be ready to move at 15 minutes notice. Short route marches, Coy & Platoon drill. Football matches and Cross country race. Concert.	
" 31st	Church Parade.	

Robert Seymour Capt. & Adjt.
9th Co. of London
(Queen Victoria's Rifles)

(9 29 6) W 3332—1107 100,000 10/13 H W V Forms/C. 2118/10.

13th Bde.

5th Div.

9th L O N D O N REGT.

FEBRUARY

....

1 9 1 5

Army Form C. 2118.

Instructions regarding War Diaries and Intelligence Summaries are contained in F. S. Regs., Part II. and the Staff Manual respectively. Title pages will be prepared in manuscript.

WAR DIARY
or
INTELLIGENCE SUMMARY.
(*Erase heading not required.*)

9th County of London (Queen Victoria's Rifles)

Hour, Date, Place	Summary of Events and Information	Remarks and references to Appendices
February 1st BAILLEUL	2½ companies occupy Trenches C Sector. 1½ coys march to DRANOUTRE.	
" 2nd DRANOUTRE	" " "	
" 3rd–9th "	" " " 3 killed 6 wounded.	
" 9th "	Relieved by 15th Inf. Bde and march into billets at BAILLEUL.	
" 10th & 11th BAILLEUL.	Companies at disposal of OC Coys. cleaning up &c.	
" 12th "	Inspection of Bn by Brig. Gen. R. v. Gowan.	
" 13th "	Companies at disposal of OC Coys. Football matches.	
" 14th "	Divine Service – Football.	
15th & 16th "	Cross country race & Football.	
" 17th & 19th "	Bn held in readiness to move at short notice. Coys carry out short route marches and Physical drill &c. Bn came under orders of 15th Inf Bde.	9th Q.V.R.
" 20th DRANOUTRE.	3 Coys took over trenches – 1 Coy and details march to DRANOUTRE.	
" 21st–23rd "	3 Coys in trenches. 1 killed 7 wounded.	
" 24th–26th "	Coys at disposal of OC Coys. Draft of 113 arrived on 24th.	
" 27th–28th "	Bn occupy trenches. 1 killed. Bn under orders of 84th Inf Bde.	

March 3rd 1915.

J. Malcolm Seymour. Capt. & Adjt.
for O.C.
9th County of London
(Queen Victoria's Rifles)

(9 29 6) W3332–1107 100,000 10/13 H W V Forms/C. 2118/10.

13th Bde.

5th Div.

9th L O N D O N REGT.

MARCH

....

1 9 1 8

Instructions regarding War Diaries and Intelligence Summaries are contained in F. S. Regs., Part II. and the Staff Manual respectively. Title pages will be prepared in manuscript.

WAR DIARY
or
INTELLIGENCE SUMMARY

(Erase heading not required.)

9th Co. of London (Queen Victoria's Rifles)

March 1915.

Army Form C. 2118.

Hour, Date, Place	Summary of Events and Information	Remarks and references to Appendices
DRANOUTRE 1.3.15	Bn in trenches at WULVERGHEM 1 officer wounded	
" 7.3.15	4 other ranks killed and 11 wounded.	
" 8.3.15	Three companies in trenches. 1 wounded	
" 9.3.15	Two " "	
" 10.3.15	One Company " "	
" 11.3.15	Battalion moved into billets at St JANS. CAPEL.	
ST JANS CAPEL 12 & 13	Coy training cleaning accoutrements &c.	
" 14.3.15	Battalion moved to ROMARIN. 2 coys in trenches (PLOEGSTEERT) and 2 in support.	
PLOEGSTEERT 17.3.15	1 killed 6 wounded.	
	Bn relieved from trenches and marched to BAILLEUL to billets.	
BAILLEUL 18–21	Coy at disposal of OC Coys.	
" 22.3.15	Battalion marched to YPRES. Quartered in Cavalry barracks.	
YPRES 23.3.15	Inspection of Bn rooms, cleaning up accoutrements.	
" 24.3.15	Two companies employed on road repairing in trench area — wounded	
" To 26.3.15	1 died of wounds. ~~[illegible]~~ 2.	
" 26.3.15	Bn into huts at OUDERDOM.	
Near OUDERDOM 27th–30th	Bn in huts, practised the assault, bomb throwing and Hand Grenade throwing.	
" 31.3.15	Bn marched to YPRES. 2 companies occupied trenches 38–40 trenches. 2 Companies quartered at Infantry Bks YPRES.	

[signature] Capt. & Adj.
for OC 9th Q.V. Rifles

1247 W 3299 200,000 (E) 8/14 J.B.C. & A. Forms/C. 2118/11.

13th Bde.
5th Div.

9th L O N D O N REGT.

APRIL

1 9 1 5

121/5268

13th Brigade

9th London (Q.V's. Rifles).

Vol V 1 – 30 . 4 . 15

Instructions regarding War Diaries and Intelligence Summaries are contained in F. S. Regs., Part II. and the Staff Manual respectively. Title pages will be prepared in manuscript.

WAR DIARY *or* INTELLIGENCE SUMMARY. 9th Q. V. Rifles for April 1915.

Army Form C. 2118.

(*Erase heading not required.*)

Hour, Date, Place	Summary of Events and Information	Remarks and references to Appendices
April 1915		
YPRES 1st to 4th	Draft of 72 N.C.O's & men arrived, A.C & Machine Gun in trenches 3 R+F killed 2 Off + 9 R+F wounded, 2 died of wounds	
5th to 9th	B+D relieve A+C – A Coy to trenches 7th. C relieves A on 9th. 2 R+F killed, 7 R+F wounded.	
10th	B.C+D relieved from trenches by 15th Bde, + the Battn march to Hutments at OUDERDOM, one R+F wounded.	
OUDERDOM 11th to 18th	Digging parties furnished for working on Ramparts at YPRES. Church parade 11th. Close order Drill, Physical exercises &c. Gun Teams occupy trenches under Bde arrangements 16th. Battn move into billets at YPRES 18th. 5 R+F wounded	
YPRES 19th	Bn parade at 7.15 a.m + proceed to dug outs Rly cutting 4 R+F wounded	
20th to 22nd	Bn leave dug outs + occupy trenches Hill 60, 2 Off killed 2 Off wounded 1 Off missing, 15 R+F killed, 107 R+F wounded. Bn relieved + addressed by Genl Sir H. Smith-Dorrien rested in Field S of VLAMERTINGHE road	
ELVERDINGHE 23rd	Marched to canal bank + remained the night	
23rd to 25th	Operations E of YSER CANAL, 2 officers wounded, 21 R+F killed, 76 R+F wounded 5 R+F missing, 6 died of wounds	
26th to 28th	Bn relieved by 12th Bde 26th + rested at ELVERDINGHE. Lt NICHOLS wounded at Bde H.Q.	
29th to 30th	Bn paraded as 2 Coys + placed under orders of K.O.Y.L.I 3 R+F killed 7 R+F wounded	

[illegible signature] Capt & Adjt for O.C. 9th Q.V. Rifles

Key to Sketch.

A. [ink blot]isused communication trench from Main comm: trench K – to ruined cottage. Drain marked on sketch runs across this trench and R.E. advice and supervision are required to deal with this – as at this point trench is very shallow. This trench requires clearing and deepening.

B. Disused communication trench running from 41 Support to Ruined Farm near Q.V.R. Batn HQ. Requires clearing.

C. Two lines of dis-used dug-outs about 5 yards apart. Each line is capable of holding about one Company after clearing has been done

D. Ruined farm near Q.V.R. Batn HQ.

E. Disused fire trench running from D to 42 Support. This is in dead ground and when cleared would accomodate ~~large number of men~~ from three to four Companies.

F. Communication trench from 41 Support to ZILLEBEKE road. This trench runs as shown on sketch herewith and not as shown on Brigade sketch map. Requires baling and clearing and deepening in parts — also, if thought advisable, connected with M by cutting across ZILLEBEKE road.

G. Small support fire trench in front of 41 — Disused and requires considerable work.

H. Existing communication trench from 39 fire trench to 41 Support.

K. Main communication trench from Q.V.R. H.Q. to fire trenches.

L About 15 yards of dis-used dug outs — in dead ground.

M. Main comm: trench from 42 Supports to 45 fire trench.

N. Disused communication trench from D rto C. Requires clearing.

R H Lindsey-Renton
Capt QVR
9-4-15

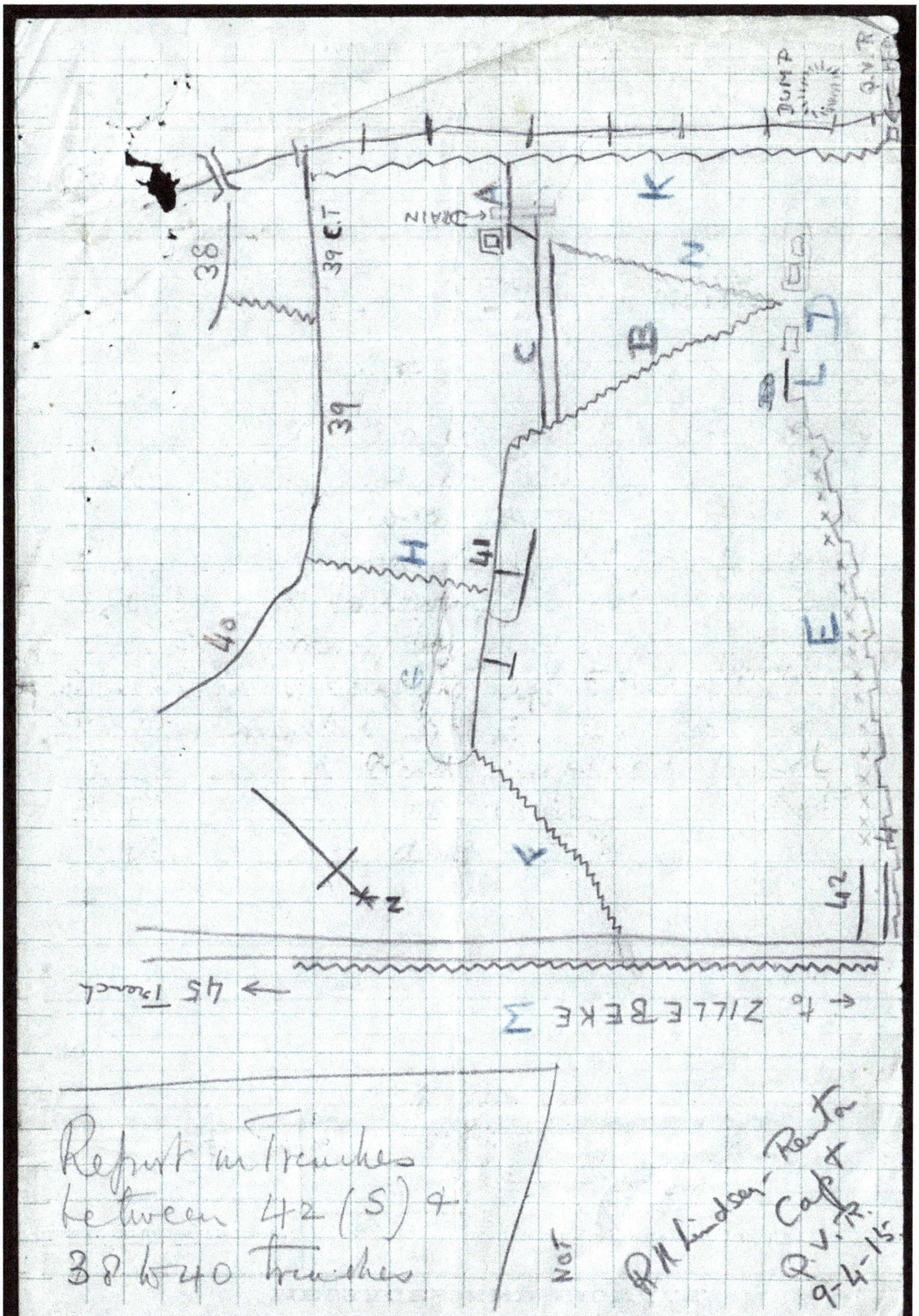

JUMP
Q.V.R.
DRAIN
38
39 C.T.
39
40
41
42
45 Trench
to ZILLEBEKE
Report on Trenches
between 42 (S) &
38 to 40 Trenches
Not
R H Lindsay-Renton
Capt
Q.V.R.
9-4-15.

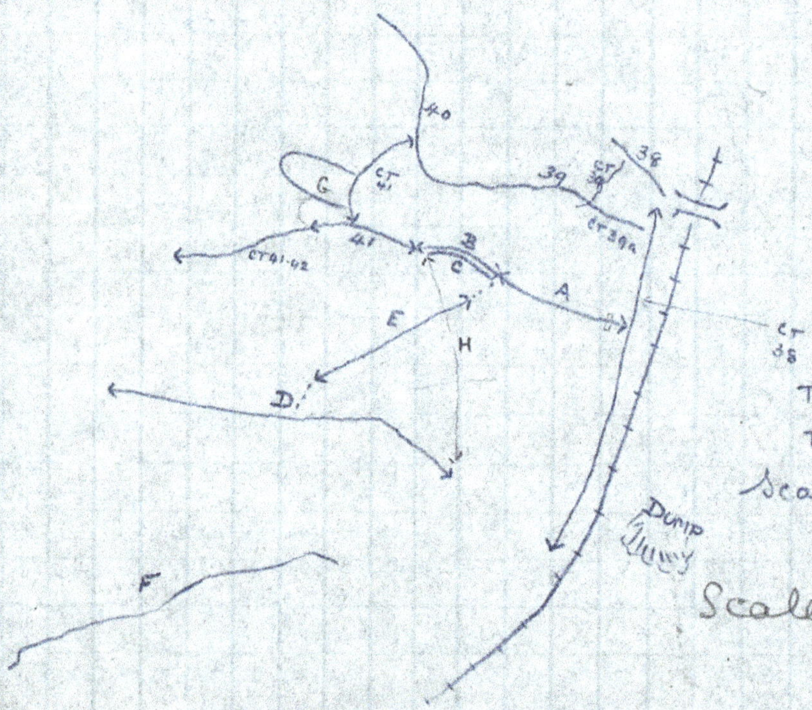

H	150
41	75
39+40	180
A	100×
BC	110× (= 2× 55)
D	250×
(E)	175×
(F)	250×
CT 39	40×
CT 39a	45×
CT 38	250×
CT 41	75×
CT 41-42	100×
TOTAL	1680×
TOTAL less E+F	1355

Scale about $\frac{1}{5,000}$

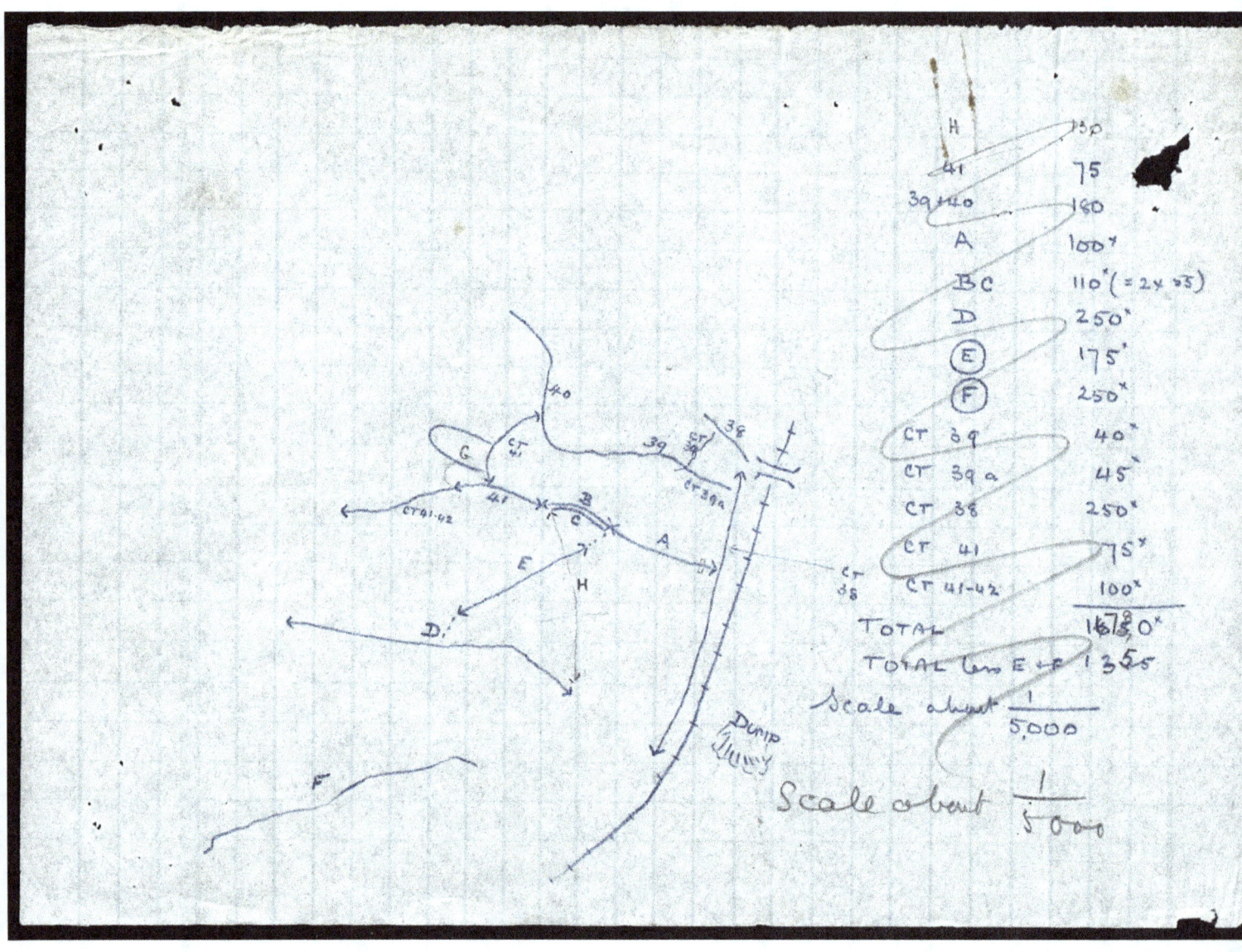

Scale about $\frac{1}{5000}$

Men	Place	Yards
(a) 200	39. 40. ½ 39a CT. 39 CT + ½ 41 CT	280
(b) 200	A. BC. ½ 41.	240
(d) 450	½ 39a CT. 38 CT ½ CT 41. ½ 41. CT 41-42 + G	525
(c) 400	H D. E.	
(e) 400	F + new trenches in rear near larch wood, larch wood dug outs etc	

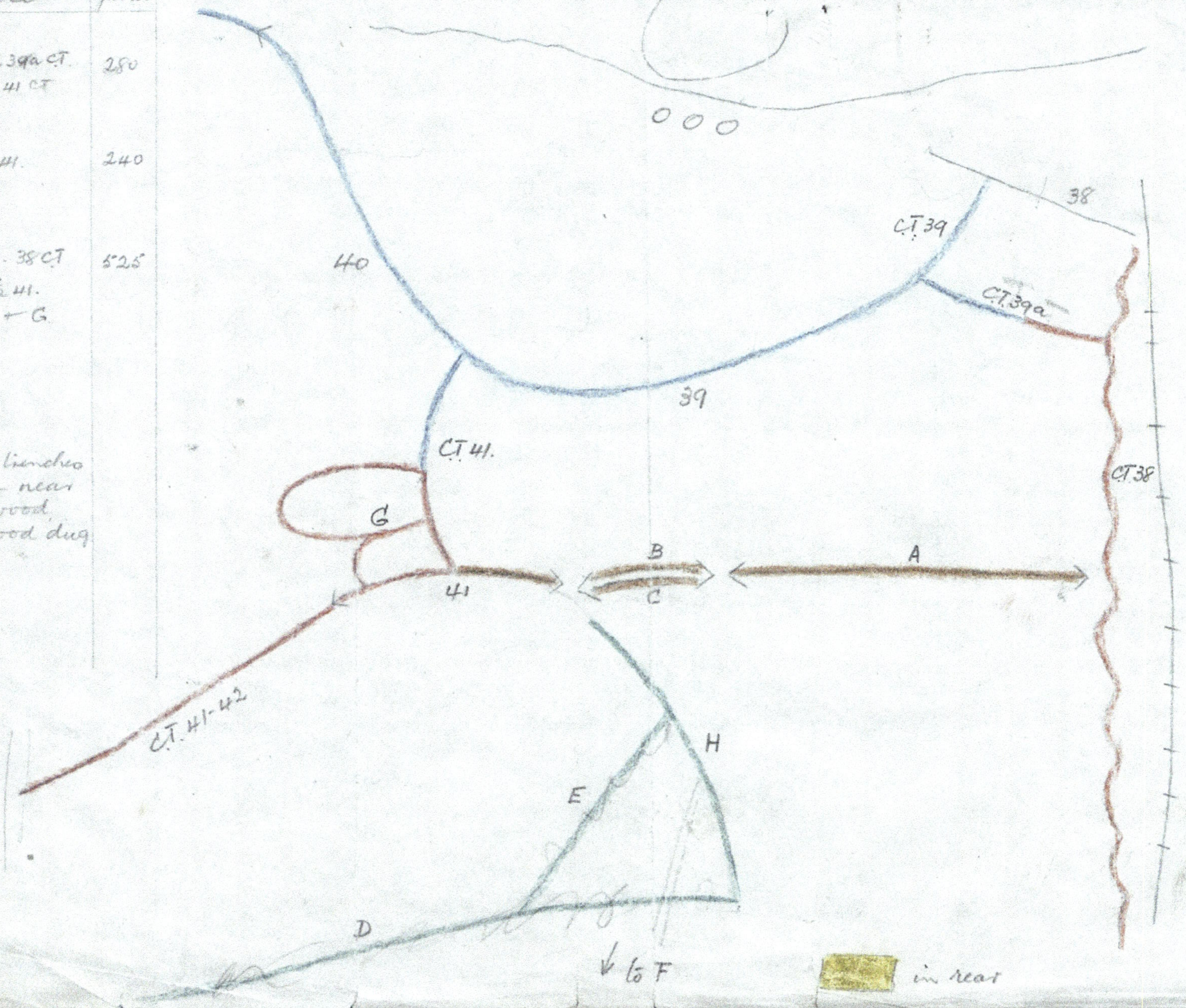

		Yards
Yards	39, 40	175
	41	80
CT	39	40
"	39a	60
"	38	225
"	41	70
"	41-42	75
	A	110
	B.C	90
	~~D~~	~~250~~
	F	125
	~~H~~	~~100~~
	~~E~~	~~120~~
	G	120

NOT to scale

13th Bde.
5th Div.

9th L O N D O N REGT.

MAY

....

1 9 1 5

Instructions regarding War Diaries and Intelligence Summaries are contained in F. S. Regs., Part II. and the Staff Manual respectively. Title pages will be prepared in manuscript.

WAR DIARY
or
INTELLIGENCE SUMMARY.
(Erase heading not required.)

Army Form C. 2118.

9th Co of London
Queen Victoria's Rifles.
1 June 1915

Hour, Date, Place		Summary of Events and Information	Remarks and references to Appendices
MAY 1915			
1	G 6. a & b	Battn moved to Wood [G 6. b] on relief from Trenches - in Bivouacs.	Map BELGIUM. Sheet 28 1:40,000.
2		Divine Service. Battn moved up into supports. 6 p.m.	
3		Bn returned 2 a.m. Into supports 5 p.m.	
4	ZEVECOTEN	Batn moved to Hutments. (Rifles (long) tested	
5	OUDERDOM	Move to F Camp. - Move off to Support Trenches & Dugouts 4 p.m.	
6	I 21. b.	Lt. Col. R. B. Shipley T.D. handed over Command of Battn to Major V. W. F. Dickins V.D.	
7		Battn in Dug-outs. providing carrying parties to Railway-cutting.	
8			
9		* Adjt (Capt G. Culme-Seymour) and 1 Rfn N.C.O. Killed - between Trenches 39 and 40.	* Morning of 7th.
10		1 Other Officer and 13 Other Ranks wounded	
11			
12		Lt. Col Commanding invalided home on 8th.	
13	SCHERPENBERG	Batn relieved at night march to SCHERPENBERG - 3 a.m. Draft of 140 N.C.Os & Men arrived	
14	"		
15	"	Rest and reorganization.	
16	"	Platoon & Coy Drill and Training.	
17	"	Musketry practice on Short range.	
18	"	Course of Instruction for Machine Gun Section.	
19	"		
20	OUDERDOM.	Sec 13-H F Camp. Company training	
21	"	" "	
22	CHATEAU BLANC (near KRUISSTRAAT.)		
23	"	In dug-outs in H 23 a & b.	
24	"	Digging and Fatigue parties of 100 per Coy provided nightly	
25	"	Casualties. 1 Officer and 21 Other Ranks wounded on Morning of 24th.	
26	VOORMEZEELE		
27	"	Battn H.Q. in Village. 3 Companies occupying Trenches Q 2 and Q 3. in	O 2. a and c
28	"	1 Company (by turn) resting in support dug outs	
29	"	in Wood 48 hours & providing carrying parties	
30	"	Casualties. Officers Nil	
31	"	Other Ranks 3 Killed & 2 wounded.	

J Chadwin Lieut. a/Adj.
for O.C. 9th Co of Lon. Q. V. Rifles

(73989) W4141—463. 400,000. 9/14. H.&J.Ltd. Forms/C. 2118/10.

13th Bde.
5th Div.

9th L O N D O N REGT.

JUNE

1 9 1 5

Instructions regarding War Diaries and Intelligence Summaries are contained in F. S. Regs., Part II. and the Staff Manual respectively. Title pages will be prepared in manuscript.

WAR DIARY
or
INTELLIGENCE SUMMARY.
(*Erase heading not required.*)

Army Form C. 2118.

9th Battn London Regt
Queen Victoria's Rifles

Hour, Date, Place		Summary of Events and Information	Arrivals.	Casualties Officers Nil. Casualties O. Ranks: Wounded	Killed	Remarks and references to Appendices
JUNE 1	VOORMEZEELE I 31 c					Map. Belgium 28 1/40000
2	"			4		
3	"			1		
4	"			7	2	
5	"			2		
6	"		2 Officers	—		
7	"			—		
8	"			2		
9	"			2	1	
10	"	Battn occupy Fire-trench Q2 Garrison 200	162 N.C.Os and Men.	—		
11	"	" " Support " Q3 " 100		2		
12	"	" Dug-outs in Wood H-35-b. Remainder of Battn		—		
13	"	Battn arranges its own reliefs - every 2nd day from		2		
14	"	1st to 10th. - every 3rd day 10 to 30th.		—		
15	"	Work - every day. Improvement of Parapets		2		
16	"	" " " C.T.s		—		
17	"	" Construction - C.T.s and Dug-outs		1		
18	"	" Nightly carrying party for Royal Engineers.		—		
19	"	Battn Hd Qrs - Convent VOORMEZEELE.				
20	"			1		
21	"			1		
22	"			—		
23	"			3		
24	"			—		
25	"			—		
26	"			1		
27	"			3		
28	"			3		
29	"			—		
30	"			—		
				2		

J Chalmers Capt & Adjt. for O.C. 9th Lon Regt

(73989) W4141—463. 400,000. 9/14. H.&J.Ltd. Forms/C. 2118/10.

13th Bde.
5th Div.

9th L O N D O N REGT.

July
....

1 9 1 5

Instructions regarding War Diaries and Intelligence Summaries are contained in F. S. Regs., Part II. and the Staff Manual respectively. Title pages will be prepared in manuscript.

WAR DIARY
or
INTELLIGENCE SUMMARY. 9th Battn Lon Regt (Queen Victorias Rifles.)

(*Erase heading not required.*)

Army Form C. 2118.

JULY	Hour, Date, Place	Summary of Events and Information	Arrivals	Casualties K.	Casualties Wd.	Remarks and references to Appendices
1						
2					1	
3					1	
4					1	
5		Battalion occupying Trench Q 2 (Fire.)			1	
6		" " Q 3 (Support)			1	
7		" " Dug-outs in Wood H. 35 b				
8		providing ~~its own~~ reliefs, carried out every 3rd night			1	
9		" carrying parties for R.E. nightly				
10						Map. BELGIUM. Sh. 28.
11	VOORMEZEELE	Work done Construction of Communication Trenches, M.G. emplacements.			8	1/40,000.
12	I 31(c)	Improvement and Drainage of Fire & Com. Trenches			2	
13		Almost entire re-construction of parapets & shelters.		1		
14		Situation quiet - except heavy shelling of Q3. early morning of 11th	10 Officers		8	
15					1	
16		Wind - always between S.E. and S.W.	50 O.Rks			
17		Rain - 10th and 17th.		1	2	
18				1	1	
19					1	
20						
21	9pm to 11pm.	Relieved by H. A. C. March to RENINGHELST, resting in huts				
22	RENINGHELST. 8pm	March to STEENVOORDE - rain falling heavily, very dark.				
23	G 34 b.					
24						
25		Company training consisting				
26	STEENVOORDE	Inspection by G.O.C. II Army; specially of Route Marching; march discipline.				Map BELGIUM.
27		Arm Drill				Sheet. HAZEBROUCK 5 A.
28		Physical "				
29						
30			1 Officer			
31	ON RAIL	Entrained at GODEWAERSVELDE " 3/4 hr for CORBIE & LA NEUVILLE. Arr. at 10.30 a.m.				Map AMIENS.

[illegible signature] Capt + Adjt for O.C. 9th Lon. [illegible]

13th Bde.
5th Div.

9th L O N D O N REGT.

AUGUST

1 9 1 5

Instructions regarding War Diaries and Intelligence Summaries are contained in F. S. Regs., Part II. and the Staff Manual respectively. Title pages will be prepared in manuscript.

Army Form C. 2118.

WAR DIARY
or
INTELLIGENCE SUMMARY. 1/9th Battn Lond. Regt (Queen Victorias Rifles)

(*Erase heading not required.*)

Hour, Date, Place	Summary of Events and Information	Drafts	Wind	Rain	Casualties	Remarks and references to Appendices
AUGUST 1915						
1. LA NEUVILLE	Company Drill, Route Marches		S.W.			Map AMIENS.
2. "			"	R.		
3. LA NEUVILLE TO RIBEMONT	Marched to RIBEMONT 11 am. Inspection of Brigade by G.O.C. XII Army Corps.		"	R.		Map AMIENS.
4. RIBEMONT TO BRAY SUR SOMME	Moved to BRAY. 8 p.m. to 12.30 am (5th)		W.			Map AMIENS
5. BRAY	Inspection + Improvement of Billets. Police-posts + Guards on Roads around BRAY, posted.	60 O.R.	S.W.			Machine Guns posted for Anti-Aircraft work.
6. "	Inspection of 2 Companies by French Generals Commanding Brigade, Division + Army Corps.		"			
7. "	Guard of Honour furnished on departure of French General NINOUS.		"			
8. "	Company Training. S.A.A. tests carried out. Swimming instruction &c.		"			
9. "	Company Training. Church Service. 2nd Lt. Lane + 2 O.R. to French Mortar Course at VALHEUREUX.		"			
10. "	Company Training. Swimming instruction &c		"	R.		
11. "	" " "		"			
12. "	" " " Lt. W. UPWARD + 2 O.R. to V Army Salvage Coy.		"	R.		
13. "	Company Training. 10 pm. 3 Offs + 75 diggers for Cable Trench		S.E.			

J. C. Andrews Capt. + Adjt.
for O.C. 1/9th Battn. Lond. Regt (Queen Victoria Rifles)

(73989) W4141—463. 400,000. 9/14. H.&J.Ltd. Forms/C. 2118/10.

Instructions regarding War Diaries and Intelligence Summaries are contained in F. S. Regs., Part II. and the Staff Manual respectively. Title pages will be prepared in manuscript.

WAR DIARY
or
INTELLIGENCE SUMMARY.
(*Erase heading not required.*)

Army Form C. 2118.

Hour, Date, Place	Summary of Events and Information	Drafts	Wind	Rain	Casualties	Remarks and references to Appendices
AUGUST 1915						
14. BRAY	Company Training		S.W.			Map AMIENS
15. BRAY to BRONFAY 8.45pm	Carrying + Mining Parties for R.E. } Nightly		W.			Mjr. Cox on Leave to England
16. BRONFAY	" " } Nightly		W.	R.		Lt. Sampson " "
17 "	" " } Nightly		N.W.	R.		Map AMIENS
18 BRONFAY to CARNOY	Moved into Trenches + Dugouts at 8.45 pm. 3 Coys A.B.C. in Trenches, D Coy in Dugouts. Relieved K.O.S.B.		"			" "
19 CARNOY	In Trenches + Dugouts. } Mining. Improvement		"			Lt. Rashleigh retd. off Leave.
20 "	" " } of Trenches + Parapets.	26 O.R.	N		4 (slight)	Gas from earth in mines.
21 "	" " } Building Dugouts.		"			
22 "	" " } Occupation of Advanced		"			2nd Lt. Richmond to Hospital.
23 "	" " } Trench + Listening Posts		"		1. O.R. Killed.	
24 "	2 Coys. withdrawn to BRAY. Trenches taken over from Devons.		"		1. O.R. " 1. O.R. Wded.	
25 "	In Trenches + Dugouts + at Bray } Improvement of		E			Mjr. Cox + Lt. Sampson returned.
26 "	" " } Trenches +		"			
27 "	" " } Parapets.		"			
28 "	" " } Building		N.W.	R.		
29 "	" " } Dugouts.		"	R.		
30 "	" " } Construction of H.Q.		S.W.			
31 "	" " } Dugout at CARNOY		"			

J. Chandeuss [signature] Capt. + Adjt.
for O.C. 1/9th Battn. Lond. Regt. (Queen Victoria Rifles)

(73989) W4141—463. 400,000. 9/14. H.&J.Ltd. Forms/C. 2118/10.

13th Bde.
5th Div.

9th L O N D O N REGT.

SEPTEMBER

1 9 1 5

Instructions regarding War Diaries and Intelligence Summaries are contained in F. S. Regs., Part II. and the Staff Manual respectively. Title pages will be prepared in manuscript.

WAR DIARY or ~~INTELLIGENCE SUMMARY.~~

1/9th Battn Lon Regt — Queen Victorias Rifles.

(Erase heading not required.)

Army Form C. 2118.

September 1915.

September	Hour, Date, Place	Summary of Events and Information	CASUALTIES OFFS.	CASUALTIES O. RANKS	WIND	RAIN	DRAFTS (~~Remarks and references to Appendices~~)
1	BRAY & CARNOY				S		
2	" "			1 Wded	S		
3	" "				SW		
4	" "	Mine exploded on neighbouring Left Front 8.30 by enemy Artillery Support		2 Killed	SW		
5	" "	1½ Coys in Billets BRAY. ½ Coy in Dug-outs CARNOY			W		C.O. to England on Leave. Major R.W. Cox in Command.
6	" "				W		
7	" "	2 Coys in Trenches 36 to 41.			NW		
8	" "	Construction of new Battn H.Q. Dug outs.			NW		
9	" "	Improvement of Fire Trenches, Parapets &c	1 Killed (Capt Holms)	1 Wded	N		
10	" "	Work for R.E.s			N		
11	" "				NE		
12	" "				NE		
13	" "	S.W.B. attached for 24 hours. Officers & N.C.O.s			W		
14	" "	Platoons		[illegible]	W		

W W F Dickins Lieut. Col.
O/C 1/9th Battn Lond. Regt. Queen Victorias Rifles

(73989) W4141—463. 400,000. 9/14. H.&J.Ltd. Forms/C. 2118/10.

Instructions regarding War Diaries and Intelligence Summaries are contained in F. S. Regs., Part II. and the Staff Manual respectively. Title pages will be prepared in manuscript.

Army Form C. 2118.

WAR DIARY or ~~INTELLIGENCE SUMMARY.~~

1/9th Battn Lond Regt — Queen Victorias Rifles.

(Erase heading not required.)

September 1915

SEPT 15	Hour, Date, Place	Summary of Events and Information	CASUALTIES OFFS.	CASUALTIES O.RKS	WIND	RAIN	DRAFTS.
15	BRAY & CARNOY	as before.			N.W.		
16	" "				N.		
17	" "	Lieut. Col. V.W.F. Dickins rejoined from leave.		1 Wded.	N.		
18	" "				N.		
19	" "				N.E.		
20	" "				N.E.		
21	" "				N.E.		
22	" "				N.E.		
23	H.Q. at BRONFAY Farm	2 Coys move to CARNOY and 2 Coys to BILLON on relief by Dorset Regt.		1 Wded.	S.E.		
24	"				S.		
25	"				S.W.		
26	"	Carrying & digging fatigues			W.		
27					N.W.		
28	"				N.W.		48 O.R.
29	"				N.		
30.	"	Battn. proceeded to billets at CHIPILLY on being relieved by 9th Gloucester Regt.		1 Killed.	N.		

V.W.F. Dickins Lieut-Col
O/C 1/9th Battn Lond Regt Queen Victorias Rifles

(73989) W4141—463. 400,000. 9/14. H.&J.Ltd. Forms/C. 2118/10.

13th Bde.
5th Div.

9th LONDON REGT.

OCTOBER

....

1 9 1 5

Instructions regarding War Diaries and Intelligence Summaries are contained in F. S. Regs., Part II. and the Staff Manual respectively. Title pages will be prepared in manuscript.

Army Form C. 2118.

WAR DIARY or ~~INTELLIGENCE SUMMARY.~~

Queen Victorias Rifles 1/9th Battn. Lond. Regt.

(Erase heading not required.)

October 1915

Place	Date	Hour	Summary of Events and Information	WIND	RAIN	CASUALTIES Officers	CASUALTIES O.R.	ARRIVALS & DEPARTURES	Remarks and references to Appendices
	1915 Oct.								
CHIPILLY	1		Company & Battalion Training. Route Marches. Practice of Attack. Road mending. (1–7)	S.W					
"	2			W					
"	3			W					
"	4			N.W	✓				
"	5			N	✓				
"	6			N					
"	7								
BRAY & ETINEHAM	8		Hd. Qrs. & 2 Coys. moved to billets at BRAY; 2 Coys. to billets at ETINEHAM.						
"	9		Mining Fatigues at FRICOURT.						
BRAY & CARNOY	10		2 Coys. moved from ETINEHAM to BRAY. Hd. Qrs. and 1/2 Coy. to dug-outs at CARNOY; 2 Coys. relieved 2/K.O.S.B. in Trenches 36 to 41.						
"	11		1½ Coys. in Billets at BRAY, ½ Coy in dug-outs at CARNOY 2 Coys. in Trenches 36 to 41. (11–12)						
"	12								
"	13		Mining & Carrying Fatigues. Construction of Battn Hd. Qrs. dug-outs at CARNOY, and of Support Line. (13–14)						
"	14						1 WDED		

W. J. Dickins Lieut-Col
O.C. Queen Victorias Rifles.

2353 Wt. W2544/1454 700,000 5/15 D. D. & L. A.D.S.S./Forms/C. 2118.

Army Form C. 2118.

Instructions regarding War Diaries and Intelligence Summaries are contained in F. S. Regs., Part II. and the Staff Manual respectively. Title pages will be prepared in manuscript.

WAR DIARY or ~~INTELLIGENCE SUMMARY.~~

Queen Victorias Rifles 1/9th Battn. Lond. Regt.

(Erase heading not required.)

October 1915

Place	Date	Hour	Summary of Events and Information	WIND	RAIN	CASUALTIES Officers	CASUALTIES O.R.	ARRIVALS & DEPARTURES	Remarks and references to Appendices
	1915 Oct.								
BRAY & CARNOY	15		Mine exploded by enemy at FRICOURT. 1 O.R. of fatigue party suffered from mine gas and shock.				1 WDED	Capt H.E.L. COX & 2/Lt. G. WOODS dep. "On Leave".	
"	16						1 KD.		
"	17								
"	18						1 WDED		
"	19		1½ Coys. in billets at BRAY. ½ Coy in dug-outs at CARNOY.					Capt. J.C. ANDREWS dep. "On Leave".	
"	20		2 Coys in Trenches 36 to 41. Mining and carrying fatigues.						
"	21		Construction of Battn. Hd. Qrs. dug-outs at CARNOY, and of						
"	22		Support Line.						
"	23			N.E.		Capt. A.E. WALLER WDED.	1 KD. 1 WDED	Capt. H.E.L. COX & 2/Lt. G. WOODS Retd. "From Leave".	
"	24			S.E.					
"	25		Mine exploded by enemy ~~at ENTONNOIRS~~. Mining fatigue party overcome by mine gas. 3 O.R. Killed, 3 O.R. suffered from gas and shock.	N.E.	1		3 KD. 3 WDED		
"	26			E			1 KD.		
"	27			E				Capt. J.C. ANDREWS Retd. "From Leave".	
"	28			E	1				

W.D.P. Dickins Lieut. Col
O.C. Queen Victorias Rifles

2353 Wt. W2544/1454 700,000 5/15 D. D. & L. A.D.S.S./Forms/C. 2118.

Instructions regarding War Diaries and Intelligence Summaries are contained in F. S. Regs., Part II. and the Staff Manual respectively. Title pages will be prepared in manuscript.

Army Form C. 2118.

WAR DIARY or ~~INTELLIGENCE SUMMARY.~~

Queen Victorias Rifles 1/9th Battn. Lond. Regt.

(Erase heading not required.)

October 1915

Place	Date	Hour	Summary of Events and Information	WIND	RAIN	CASUALTIES Officers	CASUALTIES O.R.	ARRIVALS & DEPARTURES	Remarks and references to Appendices
	1915 Oct.								
BRAY & CARNOY	29		Heavy vibration in dug-outs at CARNOY from mine exploded by enemy.	S.W	✓				
	30			S.E	✓			Maj. T. O'SHEA dep. "On Leave". Capt G.H. WOOLLEY V.C. arr. from England	
			Battalion in billets at BRAY, dug-outs at CARNOY and trenches.						
	31			S.E.					

W F Dickins Lieut. Col
O.C. Queen Victorias Rifles.

2353 Wt. W2544/1454 700,000 5/15 D. D. & L. A.D.S.S./Forms/C. 2118.

13th Bde.
5th Div.

9th L O N D O N REGT.

NOVEMBER

1 9 1 5

Army Form C. 2118.

Instructions regarding War Diaries and Intelligence Summaries are contained in F. S. Regs., Part II. and the Staff Manual respectively. Title pages will be prepared in manuscript.

Queen Victorias Rifles WAR DIARY or ~~INTELLIGENCE SUMMARY.~~ 1/9th Battn. Lond. Regt.

(Erase heading not required.)

November 1915

Place	Date	Hour	Summary of Events and Information	WIND	RAIN	CASUALTIES Officers	CASUALTIES O. Rks.	Remarks and references to Appendices
	1915 Nov.							
BRAY & CARNOY	1		1½ Coys. in Billets at BRAY, ½ Coy. in dug-outs at CARNOY, 2 Coys.	W.	✓			
	2		in Trenches 36 to 41.	N.W.	✓			
	3		K.O.Y.L.I & K.O.S.B. on left flank. 14th Brigade on right flank.	W.				
	4			N.E.				
	5			N.E.				
	6		Mining + Carrying Fatigues. Construction of Battn. Hd. Qrs. Dugouts	N.E.				
	7		at CARNOY. Trench clearing and repairing. Billet repairing at BRAY.	N.W.			1 wded.	
	8			S.				
	9			S.W.	✓			
	10			S.W.	✓			
	11			S.W.				
	12			S.W.	✓		1 Killed	
	13			W.				
	14			W				
	15			N	Snow			

W. R. Dickins Lieut.-Col.
O. C. Queen Victorias Rifles.

2353 Wt. W2544/1454 700,000 5/15 D. D. & L. A.D.S.S./Forms/C. 2118.

Instructions regarding War Diaries and Intelligence Summaries are contained in F. S. Regs., Part II. and the Staff Manual respectively. Title pages will be prepared in manuscript.

Army Form C. 2118.

Queen Victorias Rifles WAR DIARY 1/9th Battn. Lond. Regt
or
~~INTELLIGENCE SUMMARY.~~

(Erase heading not required.)

November 1915

Place	Date	Hour	Summary of Events and Information	WIND	RAIN	CASUALTIES		Remarks and references to Appendices
						Officers	O. RKS.	
BRAY & CARNOY.	1915 Nov. 16		Battalion in billets at BRAY, dug-outs at CARNOY and trenches.	S.	Snow			
	17			W.				
	18			Nil			2 wded.	
	19			N.E.				
	20			NE				
	21		Enemy Patrol of 3 men encountered. 2 Killed + 1 wounded (since died) Bodies brought in and wounded man interrogated. Very little information obtained. Regt. to which they belonged recently transferred from Russia. Equipment new. Boots good and clean. Clothing indifferent.	N.E.				
	22			N.				
	23			S				
	24			N				
	25			N			1 wded.	
	26			NE				
	27			S.E.			1 wded.	
	28			NE	✓			
	29			S				
	30.			S				

V. W. F. Dickins Lieut-Col.
O.C. Queen Victorias Rifles.

2353 Wt. W2544/1454 700,000 5/15 D. D. & L. A.D.S.S./Forms/C. 2118.

13th Bde.

5th Div.

9th LONDON REGT.

DECEMBER

1 9 1 5

Army Form C. 2118.

WAR DIARY
or
INTELLIGENCE SUMMARY.
(*Erase heading not required.*)

Instructions regarding War Diaries and Intelligence Summaries are contained in F. S. Regs., Part II. and the Staff Manual respectively. Title pages will be prepared in manuscript.

Place	Date	Hour	Summary of Events and Information	WIND	RAIN	CASUALTIES OFFICERS	CASUALTIES O. RANKS	Remarks and references to Appendices
Bray & Carnoy.	1915. DEC.							
	1		1½ Coys in Billets at BRAY, ½ Coy & Hd Qrs in dugouts at CARNOY	S	✓			
	2		2 Coys in Trenches 36 to 41	S				
	3		K.O.Y.L.I. & K.O.S.B. on left flank 14^d Brigade on right flank.	W	✓			
	4			SW				
	5			SW	✓		1 Wounded 1 (accidentally)	
	6		Mining & Carrying Fatigues. Repairing of Dugouts at CARNOY	S	✓			
	7		Trench clearing and repairing. Billet repairing at BRAY	SW	✓			
	8			NIL				
	9		Headquarter dugouts & vicinity considerably shelled with	SE	✓			
	10		light shrapnel by enemy at 11 pm (9^t) & 5 am (10^t)	S	✓			
	11			SW	✓			
	12			N	✓			
	13			N			1 Wounded.	
	14			S				
	15			S	✓			
	16			S	✓		1 accidentally killed by collapse of Dugout.	

J C Andrews Capt & Adjt
for O.C. Queen Victoria Rifles

2353 Wt. W2514/1454 700,000 5/15 D. D. & L. A.D.S.S./Forms/C. 2118.

Instructions regarding War Diaries and Intelligence Summaries are contained in F. S. Regs., Part II. and the Staff Manual respectively. Title pages will be prepared in manuscript.

WAR DIARY
or
INTELLIGENCE SUMMARY.
(Erase heading not required.)

Army Form C. 2118.

Place	Date	Hour	Summary of Events and Information	WIND	RAIN	CASUALTIES Officers	CASUALTIES O. Ranks	Remarks and references to Appendices
BRAY &	1915 Dec							
CARNOY	17		Battalion in Billets at Bray, in dugouts at Carnoy and	SE	✓		2 Wounded	
	18		in trenches 36-41	NW				
	19		Bombing Party attacked enemy M-G position, but were unsuccessful.	NW				
			Two of the party were killed, bodies being left behind & captured by			1 Wounded	2 Killed 3 Wounded	
			enemy. 1 Officer & 3 other Ranks wounded.	NE				
	20			NE				
	21			N	✓			
	22			W	✓			
	23			SW				
	24		Artillery on both sides, more active than usual.	SW				
	25			SW				
	26			SW				
	27			W				
	28			SW				
	29			S				
	30			S				

J Andrews Capt & Adjt
[illegible] Rifles

15

13th Brigade.

5th Division.

Battalion transferred to 169th Brigade.
56th Division 1st February 1916

WAR DIARY

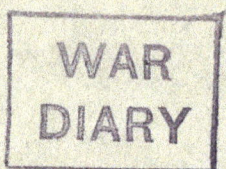

1/9th BATTALION

LONDON REGIMENT (Q.V.R.)

JANUARY 1916

56

Dw 5

13 Bde

1/9 London Regt

Jan

Vol XIV

70169 Bde Feby 1st 16.

Army Form C. 2118.

Instructions regarding War Diaries and Intelligence Summaries are contained in F. S. Regs., Part II. and the Staff Manual respectively. Title pages will be prepared in manuscript.

WAR DIARY
or
INTELLIGENCE SUMMARY.

Queen Victoria's Rifles 1/9th Battn. Lond. Regt.

(*Erase heading not required.*)

Place	Date	Hour	Summary of Events and Information	WIND	RAIN	CASUALTIES OFFICERS	CASUALTIES O.RANKS	Remarks and references to Appendices
BRAY & CARNOY	1916 JAN.							
	1		Battalion in Billets at BRAY, in dugouts at CARNOY and in	S.W			1 wounded (Slightly)	
	2		Trenches 36 - 41.	S.W.	/			
	3			N.W.			2 wounded (Slightly)	
	4		Support line considerably shelled by enemy. Billet in BRAY					
			shelled, 2 O.Rks. slightly wounded.	S.W.			2 wounded (Slightly)	
	5	→	Building and repairing dugouts in Firing Line. Fire and	N.W				
	6		Communication Trenches repaired and cleaned. Carrying fatigues.	W				
	7			S.W.	/			
	8			W	/			
	9			Nil.				Draft of 4 Officers from U.K.
	10		Battalion relieved by 2/Wilts. Hd. Qrs. and 2½ Coys. withdrawn to BRAY, less 3 Officers and small party O. Ranks left for 24 hours for instructional purposes.	W				
	11		Battalion marched from BRAY (leaving 6.15 p.m.) to billets at SAILLY LAURETTE (arriving 8.45 p.m.)	N.W.	/			Map 1/40000 ALBERT J36d-K31c.
	12			N.				

W F Dickins Lieut.-Col.
O.C. Queen Victoria's Rifles.

2353 Wt. W2544/1454 700,000 5/15 D. D. & L. A.D.S.S./Forms/C. 2118.

Instructions regarding War Diaries and Intelligence Summaries are contained in F. S. Regs., Part II. and the Staff Manual respectively. Title pages will be prepared in manuscript.

WAR DIARY
or
INTELLIGENCE SUMMARY.
(Erase heading not required.)

Army Form C. 2118.

Place	Date	Hour	Summary of Events and Information		Remarks and references to Appendices
	1916 JAN.				
SAILLY LAURETTE	13		Company close order, open order and arm drill. Route marches.		
	14		Practise of attack by Battalion. Bombing and musketry practise.		Draft of 4 Officers from U.K.
	15		Instructional class for Junior Officers and N.C.Os		
	16				Draft of 1 Officer from U.K.
	17				
	18				
	19				
	20				
	21				Draft of 95 O.R. from No. 4 Ent. Batt.
	22				
	23				Draft of 19 O.R. from No. 9 Ent. Batt.
	24				
	25				
	26				
	27				
	28.				

W P Dickins Lieut.-Col.
O.C. Queen Victorias Rifles.

2353 Wt. W2544/1454 700,000 5/15 D. D. & L. A.D.S.S./Forms/C. 2118.

Army Form C. 2118.

WAR DIARY
or
INTELLIGENCE SUMMARY.
(Erase heading not required.)

Instructions regarding War Diaries and Intelligence Summaries are contained in F. S. Regs., Part II. and the Staff Manual respectively. Title pages will be prepared in manuscript.

Place	Date	Hour	Summary of Events and Information	Remarks and references to Appendices
SAILLY LAURETTE	1916 JAN 29			Draft of 1 Officer from U.K.
LA HOUSSOYE	30		Battalion marched from SAILLY LAURETTE (leaving 9.0 am) to billets in LA HOUSSOYE (arriving at 12.45 pm)	Map $\frac{1}{100000}$ AMIENS 12. F 1.
TALMAS	31		Battalion marched from LA HOUSSOYE (leaving 9.0 am. to billets in TALMAS (arriving at 1.40 pm.) 14/Warwicks in neighbouring billets.	$\frac{1}{100000}$ LENS Sheet 11. D.6.

F W P Dickins Lieut.-Col.
O.C. Queen Victoria's Rifles

2353 Wt. W2544/1454 700,000 5/15 D. D. & L. A.D.S.S./Forms/C. 2118.

www.ingramcontent.com/pod-product-compliance
Lightning Source LLC
Chambersburg PA
CBHW082007220426
43670CB00014B/2572
* 9 7 8 1 4 7 4 5 0 5 8 0 2 *